The Web
of Belief

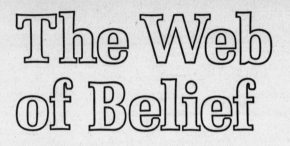

The Web of Belief

SECOND EDITION

by
W. V. QUINE
Harvard University

J. S. ULLIAN
Washington University

RANDOM HOUSE　NEW YORK

Second Edition

9 8 7 6 5 4 3 2 1

Copyright © 1970, 1978 by Random House, Inc.

Library of Congress Cataloging in Publication Data
Quine, Willard Van Orman.
    The web of belief.

    Bibliography: p.
    Includes index.
1. Belief and doubt. 2. Reasoning. I. Ullian,
J. S., 1930–   joint author. II. Title.
BD215.Q5 1978   121'.6   77-14473
ISBN 0-394-32179-0

Manufactured in the United States of America

Book design by Brenda Kamen

Preface

This little book is a compact introduction to the study of rational belief. It is meant to afford a coherent view of a broad philosophical terrain, providing points of entry to such areas of philosophy as theory of knowledge, methodology of science, and philosophy of language.

It was commissioned eleven years ago for inclusion in a series intended for freshman courses in English. The first edition appeared in 1970. To our surprise it made its way mainly into introductory philosophy courses. Revising it in the light of this trend, we have at points allowed ourselves a more frankly philosophical tone than before and have developed philosophical themes a little further. We have been able to assume that our readers will be more tolerant of philosophical lucubrations than we dared assume before. We have aimed still at undergraduates generally, regardless of department, and have presupposed no philosophical training. But we have tried to encourage interest in philosophy.

The book is a little longer than before, and almost half of it is rewritten. The most central chapter, "Hypothesis," has been reorganized and tightened. The chapter on Explanation has been almost wholly rewritten, to present a less perfunctory doctrine than before. Five pages have been added on Evaluation, a topic previously touched only lightly. Paragraphs sparked by the latter-day resurgence of irrationalism have found their way into the new Introduction and into various of the subsequent chapters. Many passages have been revised for enhancement of clarity. A Glossary and an Index have been added.

We are grateful to Professors J. J. C. Smart and Edwin Martin, Jr. for helpful criticism of several points in the first edition. And we are indebted most particularly to Professor Douglas Stalker, who provided us with a constructive and painstaking criticism of the first edition, much of it page by page. He had been teaching from the book, and his penetrating comments and suggestions revealed remarkable pedagogical gifts and dedication as well as sound philosophy. Much of our revision was guided by his comments. Of equal importance, in spurring us to new efforts, was simply the awareness that our little book was receiving such serious and respectful scrutiny in so competent a quarter.

W. V. Q.
J. S. U.

Contents

The Web of Belief

Chapter I

Introduction

Our word "science" comes from a Latin word for knowledge. Much that we know does not count as science, but this is often less due to its subject matter than to its arrangement. For nearly any body of knowledge that is sufficiently organized to exhibit appropriate evidential relationships among its constituent claims has at least some call to be seen as scientific. What makes for science is system, whatever the subject. And what makes for system is the judicious application of logic. Science is thus a fruit of rational investigation.

The scientific community is no private club. In principle, and in the best and broadest sense of the words, scientific inquiry can be undertaken by anyone on almost any subject matter. Practically speaking, such inquiry often demands a vast fund of background knowledge and a sizable team of cooperating inquirers, not to mention sophisticated equipment; this is because human knowledge has already progressed so far. But at root what is needed for scientific inquiry is just receptivity to data, skill in reasoning, and yearning for truth. Admittedly, ingenuity can help too.

Of course science is not the only discipline that brings enlightenment; literature and the arts teach us too. One pities the person who derives nothing from poetry or music. It has been supposed by many that appreciation of the arts bears little relation to knowledge as such, as if appreciation springs from the heart while knowledge resides in the brain. But some recent writers, like Nelson Goodman, have argued convincingly that such appreciation has a much more substantial cognitive component than has been widely realized. "Cognitive", we note, comes from a Latin word for acquiring knowledge or coming to know.

But even as light is opposed by darkness, science and reason have their enemies. Superstition and belief in magic are as old as man himself; for the intransigence of facts and our limitations in controlling them can be powerfully hard to take. Add to this the reflection that we are in an age when it is popular to distrust whatever is seen as the established view or the Establishment, and it is no wonder that anti-rational attitudes and doctrines are mustering so much support. Still, we can understand what encourages the anti-rationalist turn without losing our zeal for opposing it. A current Continuing Education catalogue offers a course description, under the heading "Philosophy", that typifies the dark view at its darkest: "Children of science that we are, we have based our cultural patterns on logic, on the cognitive, on the verifiable. But more and more there has crept into current research and study the haunting suggestion that there are other kinds of knowledge unfathomable by our cognition, other ways of knowing beyond the limits of our logic, which are deserving of our serious attention." Now "knowledge unfathomable by our cognition" is simply incoherent, as attention to the words makes clear. Moreover, all that creeps is not gold. One wonders how many students enrolled.

Not that soberly seeking to learn is all there should be; let there be fun and games as well. But let it also be clear where the boundaries are. A person might have a moderately amusing time playing with a ouija board, but if he drifts into the belief that it is a *bona fide* avenue to discovery then something has gone amiss. We will not pursue the possible socio-benefits of anti-rational doctrines; in our eyes, much better escapes from reality are available, if that's what's wanted. In the chapters ahead we will be interested in the ways of acquiring and sustaining right beliefs, be they pleasant or painful.

The avowedly anti-rational doctrines are fairly easy to spot; what can be harder is seeing which doctrines are only masquerading as science. There has been a proliferation of masqueraders of late, though the most renowned, astrology and numerology, have been with us since antiquity. But now there are biorhythms and engrams to bolster a store already bulging with orgon boxes and dowsing rods, to cite just a few pretenders. And each elaborate doctrine has or has had its swarm of devout followers. How does this happen, if the doctrines are so wrong?

The basic reasons are fairly obvious. For one thing, much science has grown so sophisticated that its practice is out of reach for most of us. To be a solid state physicist or nuclear biologist you need years of training; nor do you need much less for medicine or experimental psychology. Accordingly, what we hear from specialists in such fields is often hard for us to comprehend. It is as if they speak a different language. But even more to the point, for all their alleged expertise and renown there are basic questions that they are unable to answer—conspicuously on such vital subjects as disease and emotional disorder. Ig-

norance on these matters can be frightening. And the
response to fright is frequently to pursue whatever course
offers hope of relief from it, without pausing to examine
credentials.

And so come the cults, claiming to meet the needs that
science has thus far failed to meet—and offering the pro-
spective inductee a place on the ground floor. Some cults
may be harmless enough, but whenever false doctrine is
propagated there is some cost. Many such doctrines are
dressed up as sciences in their own right. For even though
established science may be distrusted, "science" is still a
thumbs-up word for most people. So we find many of
these theories borrowing liberally from genuine science,
and many more using terms that sound, to the uninitiated,
like the stuff of which true science is made. Now many of
the bogus doctrines are actually unintelligible; their
seeming content simply vanishes when closely scruti-
nized. But given the incomprehensibility of so much genuine science for so many of us, that very unintelligibility
can be mistaken as a sign of authenticity. Alas, it can even
inspire reverence.

Often such doctrines are accompanied by defiant attacks
on the scientific establishment. Science is said to be in the
hands of vested interests. Now there have indeed been
vested interests that have blocked progress; so such attacks can strike a responsive chord. But there seems to be
no end to how far such accusations can go. Not long ago
there was a pamphlet available that "proved" π to be expressible as a fraction. The scientific aristocracy, so it
claimed, had had its purposes in suppressing this result.
But now, for a small price, the truth was out.

When it is a mathematical truth that is assailed there
is likely to be a definitive way of settling the issue; so,
happily, it is with π. For many doctrines, though, there
is this protective argument: you (pointing to the follower

of the scientific establishment) can't disprove it! And to be sure, many of these theories that lie on or beyond the fringe of believability cannot be definitively shown to be wrong. Indeed many of them are cast in terms that are so cloudy that it is hard to know what would count as a refutation of them; for they are not intelligible in the first place. And here the naivete of the believer may blend with his instinct for giant-killing. He thinks that the fact that his belief can't be knocked all the way over is additional ground for embracing it; and he may rejoice in finding that all the mighty scientists can't put him down. A victory, of sorts, over those in power.

Many theories, good and bad, do not admit of absolute proof or disproof; we will soon be stressing some of the reasons why this is so. Sadly, it is not just false science that has wantonly traded on this. A few years ago there were large advertisements in major newspapers in which cigaret manufacturers proudly announced that they were about to have independent researchers prove that there was not, after all, any causal connection between cigaret smoking and lung cancer. Evidence amassed in support of the connection was already overwhelming, and it should have been acknowledged as such. But, grasping at the realization that a causal connection had not been shown to exist with absolute certainty, these advertisers were magnifying the less than reasonable residual doubt into a proclamation of confidence in the opposite claim. Moreover, the very attitude of proper science was perverted by what they promised; for proper science aims at truth wherever it lies, rather than at support for a profitable industry.

Our train of thought, we notice, has led us to show some signs of distrust ourselves. And we have all but pointed a finger at some vested interests! Sometimes, we admit, it is warranted. And sometimes, whatever their motives, even eminent persons of science turn out to have been wrong all along. In science, as elsewhere, use of the soundest methods does not bestow a guarantee that viable theory will accrue. Nor, it should be said, does improper method, even combined with the lowest of motives, altogether preclude arrival at truth. But it makes it very unlikely.

In the chapters ahead we will broach many of the criteria by which reasonable belief may be discriminated from unreasonable belief. But not only are the criteria not foolproof; they do not always even point in a unique direction. When we meet the Virtues for assessing hypotheses we will find that they require us to look at candidates for belief in multiple ways, to weigh together a variety of considerations. Decisions in science, as in life, can be difficult. There is no simple touchstone for responsible belief.

Chapter II

Belief and Change of Belief

One's repertoire of beliefs changes in nearly every waking moment. The merest chirp of a bird or chug of a passing motor, when recognized as such, adds a belief to our fluctuating store. These are trivial beliefs, quickly acquired and as quickly dropped, crowded out, forgotten. Other beliefs endure: the belief that Hannibal crossed the Alps, the belief that Neptune is a planet. Some of one's beliefs are at length surrendered not through just being crowded out and forgotten, but through being found to conflict with other beliefs, new ones perhaps, whose credentials seem superior. It is this need to resolve conflicts that prompts us to assess the grounds of belief, and so to turn to such reflections as will mainly occupy us in these pages.

Let us consider, to begin with, what we are up to when we believe. Just what are we doing? Nothing in particular. For all the liveliness of fluctuation of beliefs, believing is not an activity. It is not like scansion or long division. We may scan a verse quickly or slowly. We may perform a division quickly or slowly. We may even be quick or slow about coming to believe something, and quick or slow about giving a belief up. But there is nothing quick or slow about the believing itself; it is not a job to get on with. Nor is it a fit or mood, like joy or grief or astonishment. It is not something that we feel while it lasts. Rather, believing is a disposition that can linger latent and unobserved. It is a disposition to respond in certain ways when the appropriate issue arises. To believe that Hannibal crossed the Alps is to be disposed, among other things, to say "Yes" when asked. To believe that frozen foods will thaw on the table is to be disposed, among other things, to leave such foods on the table only when one wants them thawed.

Inculcating a belief is like charging a battery. The battery is thenceforward disposed to give a spark or shock, when suitably approached, as long as the charge lasts; similarly the believer is disposed to respond in characteristic ways, when suitably approached, as long as the belief lasts. The belief, like the charge, may last long or briefly. Some beliefs, like the one about Hannibal, we shall probably retain while we live. Some, like our belief in the dependability of our neighborhood cobbler, we may abandon tomorrow in the face of adverse evidence. And some, like the belief that a bird chirped within earshot, will simply die of unimportance forthwith. The belief that the cobbler is dependable gives way tomorrow to a contrary belief, while the belief in the bird is just forgotten. A disposition has ceased in both cases, though in different ways.

Grammatically the verb "believes" is transitive, like "kicks" or "drives". We say "He believes it" just as we say "He kicks it," "He drives it." This circumstance could tempt one to think of belief as an activity, which we saw it is not. But it can still raise a philosophical question as to the nature of the objects of belief. The object kicked may be a ball or a donkey; the object driven may be a car or a donkey; but what sort of object is believed? Something intangible, evidently; something named by prefixing the word 'that' to a subordinate sentence. We believe *that* Hannibal crossed the Alps. We believe *that* Neptune is a planet. What manner of thing is this believed thing—*that* Hannibal crossed the Alps? To say that it is just the sentence itself seems mistaken. Foreign speakers, after all, are said to share the belief that Hannibal crossed the Alps, even when they do not understand the English sentence. We also like to attribute a belief to a dumb animal, on the strength of his dispositions. So with the dog who wags his tail at the sound of a car in the driveway. And we sometimes even like to distinguish two beliefs when the sentence is one; for instance, the sentence "I am Napoleon" expresses different beliefs about Napoleon when uttered by different patients. Therefore, one tends to conclude that the things believed are not the sentences themselves. What then are they?

This, like various other philosophical questions, is better deflected than met head on. Instead of worrying about the simple verb "believes", as relating persons to some manner of believed things, we can retreat to the word-pair "believes true" as relating men directly to sentences. We can retreat to this without claiming that believed things are sentences; we can simply waive that claim, and the philosophical question behind it. After all, our factual interest in what some speaker of English believes is fully satisfied by finding out what sentences the speaker believes to be true.

And what criterion have we for saying that someone believes a sentence to be true? For most purposes the criterion is the obvious one: he or she assents to the sentence when asked. The criterion can fail if the person either does not understand our language or chooses to deceive us. Also the criterion is inadequate to the purposes of a psychiatrist who wants to provide for some manner of unapprehended belief or disbelief. But it is perhaps criterion enough for us.

To be quite exact, "believes true" should be seen as relating persons not to sentences but to individual acts of sentence utterance. For, as illustrated by "I am Napoleon" or "The door is open," one utterance of a sentence can be true and another false. In general, however, it is easier to specify a sentence, simply by quoting it, than to specify some individual act of utterance. So let us continue to speak simply of sentences as true and as believed true, except where confusion threatens.

For that matter, where no confusion threatens, it will be convenient and natural to go on speaking even in the old way of what a person believes, instead of what the person believes true. But whenever we are threatened by the philosophical question of objects of belief, we can gratefully retreat to the more explicit idiom which speaks of believing sentences true, or, ultimately, of believing utterances true.

It is important to distinguish between disbelief and nonbelief—between believing a sentence false and merely not believing it true. Disbelief is a case of belief; to believe a sentence false is to believe the negation of the sentence true. We disbelieve that there are ghosts; we believe that there are none. Nonbelief is the state of suspended judgment: neither believing the sentence true nor believing it false. Such is our attitude toward there being an even number of Paul Smiths in Boston. This is still nothing so contentious as believing the sentence to be neither true nor false; on the contrary, it is simply the absence of opinion.

English usage is perverse on the point: we say, confusingly, the weaker "I don't believe so" to mean the stronger "I believe not." But the fact is, taking any sentence at random, that belief and disbelief are less usual than nonbelief. Are there an even number of Paul Smiths in Boston? Will it rain in Pontiac next Labor Day? English being what it is, we answer "I don't know," because it would be misleading to say "I don't believe so." But our state is simple nonbelief.

The flight to "I don't know" compounds the perversity of idiom, for knowing is quite a special kind of believing; you can believe without knowing. Believing something does not count as knowing it unless what is believed is in fact true. And even if what is believed is true, believing it does not count as knowing it unless the believer has firm grounds for belief. Emily knows that her name is "Emily", having had firm and abundant evidence of it over the years. We must still count her as knowing it even though she cannot remember the evidence now. But Emily may merely believe and not know that the mayor is corrupt, corrupt though he is; for Emily has read only the innuendoes of the rival candidate.

In some aberrant uses that pretend to be especially deep, the words "knowledge" and "truth" become tinged with a mystical aura. There need be no mystery about either one of them. Truth is a property of sentences; it is the trait shared equally by all that would be rightly affirmed. And knowledge, in its clearest sense, is what we have of those truths if our beliefs are solidly enough grounded. As an aspiration, knowledge is in some ways like a good golf score: each is substantially the fruit of something else, and there are no magic shortcuts to either one. To improve your golf score you work at perfecting the various strokes; for knowledge you work at garnering and sifting evidence and sharpening your reasoning skills. Your immediate concern must be with the comprehensiveness and coherence of your belief body. Knowledge is no more thus guaranteed than is the lowered golf score, but there is no better way. Perhaps philosophers have done us a disservice by focusing so much on knowledge and so little on belief.

Another irregularity of English usage is a hyperbolic use of "know" as an emphatic variant of "believe". "I know the tornado will hit us," uttered with a shudder, carries less conviction than the modest declaration "I believe the tornado will hit us." Knowledge is a laudable aspiration, and speculation is laudable too as long as we are aware of what we are doing. And between these termini, inclusive, there stretches our whole fluctuating spectrum of beliefs.

A person need never have assessed the evidence for anything in order to be rich in opinion. On the contrary. Sometimes, sad to say, one even goes on assenting to sentences that contradict one another. This, however, is because inconsistency is not always obvious. We can no longer believe all of a set of sentences to be true once we know them to be in contradiction with one another, since contradiction requires one or another of them to be false. Once we recognize a conflict among our beliefs, it is up to us to gather and assess our evidence with a view to weeding out one or another of the conflicting beliefs.

Among our beliefs there are some of higher order—beliefs about beliefs—that often guide us in these assessments of evidence. We all hold, for example, that those gained from respected encyclopedias and almanacs are more to be relied on than those gained from television commercials. Further, we agree that what we think we see is usually there. Seeing is not quite believing, but it goes a long way.

Evidence for belief must be distinguished from causes of belief; for some causes of belief can be counted as evidence and some cannot. The cause of a belief may have been some unqualified person's irresponsible remark. It may even have been a misunderstanding on our part of someone's words, or a subconscious association of ideas. Its effectiveness may have been enhanced by wishful thinking. The cause may have gone unnoticed, or have been forgotten; but the belief is there, and by chance it may even be true. On a later occasion we may gather evidence to defend it.

What we call hunches from out of nowhere probably spring from unnoticed stimulations. In many cases the forgotten or unnoticed cause of a belief may have constituted quite good evidence in its own right, and it is only because of our inability to retrieve that cause that we have later to seek fresh evidence in defense of the belief. Sounds in the night, not even consciously detected, may have caused our belief that our fraternity brother got back from his revels. The sounds not only caused our belief, but were fair evidence; yet the first evidence we are able to cite may come only the next morning when we see his sports car in the drive.

As long as a belief whose causes are undetected is not challenged by other persons, and engenders no conflict that would prompt us to wonder about it ourselves, we are apt to go on holding it without thought of evidence. This practice is often reasonable, time being limited. But it remains important to keep in mind that cause is commonly quite another thing than evidence. One obvious test of evidence is this: would it still be taken to support the belief if we stripped away all motives for wanting the belief to be true? As long as we see cause clearly as cause and only evidence as evidence, we remain alert for any hint that the time has come when the evidence for one of our beliefs should be sought and sifted. Also we become less susceptible to some of the causes of belief that have nothing to do with evidence, such as the catchiness of an advertising jingle.

The intensity of a belief cannot be counted on to reflect its supporting evidence any more than its causes can. We may have little support for a belief tightly held, or much support for some belief that has not yet dawned upon us. In the goodness of her heart some dear old soul may retain implicit faith in the probity of her brisk family solicitor, though, if she would only put two and two together, she has clear evidence that he is mercilessly bilking her of her paltry patrimony. Insofar as we are rational in our beliefs, however, the intensity of belief will tend to correspond to the firmness of the available evidence. Insofar as we are rational, we will drop a belief when we have tried in vain to find evidence for it.

Often in assessing beliefs we do best to assess several in combination. A very accomplished mechanic might be able to tell something about an automobile's engine by examining its parts one by one, each in complete isolation from the others, but it would surely serve his purpose better to see the engine as a whole with all the parts functioning together. So with what we believe. It is in the light of the full body of our beliefs that candidates gain acceptance or rejection; any independent merits of a candidate tend to be less decisive. To see why this should be, recall the characteristic occasion for questioning beliefs. It was the situation where a new belief, up for adoption, conflicts somehow with the present body of beliefs as a body. Now when a set of beliefs is inconsistent, at least one of the beliefs must be rejected as false; but a question may remain open as to which to reject. Evidence must then be assessed, with a view to rejecting the least firmly supported of the conflicting beliefs. But even that belief will have had some supporting evidence, however shaky; so in rejecting it we may have to reject also some tenuous belief that had helped to support it. Revision may thus progress downward as the evidence thins out.

Let Abbott, Babbitt, and Cabot be suspects in a murder case. Abbott has an alibi, in the register of a respectable hotel in Albany. Babbitt also has an alibi, for his brother-in-law testified that Babbitt was visiting him in Brooklyn at the time. Cabot pleads alibi too, claiming to have been watching a ski meet in the Catskills, but we have only his word for that. So we believe

(1)   that Abbott did not commit the crime,
(2)   that Babbitt did not,
(3)   that Abbott or Babbitt or Cabot did.

But presently Cabot documents his alibi—he had the good luck to have been caught by television in the sidelines at the ski meet. A new belief is thus thrust upon us:

(4)   that Cabot did not.

Our beliefs (1) through (4) are inconsistent, so we must choose one for rejection. Which has the weakest evidence? The basis for (1) in the hotel register is good, since it is a fine old hotel. The basis for (2) is weaker, since Babbitt's brother-in-law might be lying. The basis for (3) is perhaps twofold: that there is no sign of burglary and that only Abbott, Babbitt, and Cabot seem to have stood to gain from the murder apart from burglary. This exclusion of burglary seems conclusive, but the other consideration does not; there could be some fourth beneficiary. For (4), finally, the basis is conclusive: the evidence from television. Thus (2) and (3) are the weak points. To resolve the inconsistency of (1) through (4) we should reject (2) or (3), thus either incriminating Babbitt or widening our net for some new suspect.

See also how the revision progresses downward. If we
reject (2), we also revise our previous underlying belief,
however tentative, that the brother-in-law was telling the
truth and Babbitt was in Brooklyn. If instead we reject (3),
we also revise our previous underlying belief that none
but Abbott, Babbitt, and Cabot stood to gain from the
murder apart from burglary.

Finally a certain arbitrariness should be noted in the
organization of this analysis. The inconsistent beliefs (1)
through (4) were singled out, and then various further
beliefs were accorded a subordinate status as underlying
evidence: a belief about a hotel register, a belief about the
prestige of the hotel, a belief about the television, a perhaps unwarranted belief about the veracity of the brother-
in-law, and so on. We could instead have listed this full
dozen of beliefs on an equal footing, appreciated that they
were in contradiction, and proceeded to restore consistency by weeding them out in various ways. But the organization lightened our task: it focused our attention on
four prominent beliefs among which to drop one, and then
it ranged the other beliefs under these four as mere aids
to choosing which of the four to drop.

The strategy illustrated would seem in general to be a
good one: divide and conquer. When a set of beliefs has
accumulated to the point of contradiction, find the small-
est selection of them you can that still involves contradiction; for instance, (1) through (4). For we can be sure that
we are going to have to drop some of the beliefs in that
subset, whatever else we do. In reviewing and comparing
the evidence for the beliefs in the subset, then, we will
find ourselves led down in a rather systematic way to
other beliefs of the set. Eventually we find ourselves dropping some of them too.

In probing the evidence, where do we stop? In probing
the evidence for (1) through (4) we dredged up various

underlying beliefs, but we could have probed further, seeking evidence in turn for them. In practice the probing stops when we are satisfied how best to restore consistency: which ones to discard among the beliefs we have canvassed.

Our adjustment of an inconsistent set of beliefs may be either decisive or indecisive. If it is decisive, each belief of the set is either kept or switched to disbelief. If it is indecisive, some of the beliefs simply give way to nonbelief; judgment on them is suspended. In the above example, one decisive adjustment would be to keep (1), (3), and (4), deny (2), and thus incriminate Babbitt. Another would be to keep (1), (2), and (4) and deny (3). This would again be decisive so far as concerns (1) through (4), though it would leave the murder unsolved. An indecisive adjustment would be to keep (1) and (4) but simply suspend judgment regarding (2) and (3). On the meager data before us, the most reasonable course would seem to be to rest with this indecisive outcome pending further findings.

Chapter III

Observation

The structure seen in our murder mystery is seen also in the predictions and the checking operations that are so common in science and in everyday thinking. When our system of beliefs supports our expectation of some event and that event does not occur, we have the problem of selecting certain of our interlocking beliefs for revision. This is what happens when an experiment is made to check a scientific theory and the result is not what the theory predicted. The scientist then has to revise his theory somehow; he must drop some one or another, at least, of the beliefs which together implied the false prediction. This is also what happens, less formally, whenever something expected fails to happen; we are called upon to go back and revise one or another of the beliefs which, taken together, had engendered the false expectation.

The pattern is simply that, again, of the foregoing murder mystery. For our false expectation was a belief, like our false suspicion of Cabot; and the disbelief which has superseded it creates an inconsistency in the system. Toward settling just which beliefs to give up, we consider what beliefs had mainly underlain the false prediction, and what further beliefs had underlain these, and so on, as in the murder case. We stop such probing of evidence, as was remarked, when we are satisfied.

Some of us are more easily satisfied than others. Each of us is more easily satisfied on some issues than on others: more easily satisfied on the issues that matter less. But there is a limit: when we get down to our own direct observation, there is nowhere deeper to look. Someone else's report, even of direct observation, has not quite this finality for us. We may have good reason to trust such a report, but in trusting it we are making an inference from other evidence, other observations of our own. What we are directly observing is rather the report itself, the spoken or written words. We have then to draw on past linguistic experience of the veracity of this or other speakers. A memory or even a written record of our own direct observation is still at some remove from the original observation itself, though we can seldom ask better. What we are directly observing in the case of our own written record is, like our friend's report, only inferentially related to our original observation; though in our own case we have the best of reasons to abide by the inference.

Thus the ultimate evidence that our whole system of beliefs has to answer up to consists strictly of our own direct observations—including our observations of our notes and of other people's reports. Naturally we leave many points unchecked. Lore is handed down from our forebears. Such actual evidence as any one of us does have, however, is in the end the direct evidence of the senses. Likewise such evidence as there is and ever was, collectively, for the whole overwhelming edifice of science, has consisted only in the direct evidence of many peoples' senses.

The world with its quarks and chromosomes, its distant lands and spiral nebulae, is like a vast computer in a black box, forever sealed except for its input and output registers. These we directly observe, and in the light of them we speculate on the structure of the machine, the universe. Thus it is that we think up the quarks and chromosomes, the distant lands and the nebulae; they would account for the observable data. When an observation turns out unexpectedly, we may try modifying our theory of that structure at one or another point.

When an observation shows that a system of beliefs must be overhauled, it leaves us to choose which of those interlocking beliefs to revise; this important fact has come up repeatedly. The beliefs face the tribunal of observation not singly but in a body. But note now that the observation sentence itself, the sentence that reports or predicts a present or imminent observation, is peculiar on this score. It does face the tribunal singly, in the usual case, and simply stands or falls with the observation that it reports or predicts. And, standing or falling, it sustains or lets down the system of beliefs that implied it.

What are observations? Some philosophers have taken them to be sensory events: the occurrence of smells, feels, noises, color patches. This way lies frustration. What we ordinarily notice and testify to are rather the objects and events out in the world. It is to these that our very language is geared, because language is a social institution, learned from other people who share the scene to which the words refer. Observation sentences, like theoretical sentences, are for the most part sentences about external objects. This is why they can enter into logical relations with scientific theory, confirming or refuting it.

In an early page we asked what sorts of things were the objects of belief. Then we gratefully dropped that question, noticing that we could instead talk of sentences and of believing them true. Now a similar maneuver conduces to clarity in dealing with the notion of observation: let us ask no longer what counts as an observation, but turn rather to language and ask what counts as an observation sentence.

What makes a sentence an observation sentence is not what sort of event or situation it describes, but how it describes it. Thus I may see the dean of the law school mail a birthday check to his daughter in Belgium. Saying so in these terms does not qualify as an observation sentence. If on the other hand I describe that same event by saying that I saw a stout man with a broad face, a gray moustache, rimless spectacles, a Homburg hat, and a walking stick, putting a small white flat flimsy object into the slot of a mailbox, this is an observation sentence. What makes it an observation sentence is that any second witness would be bound to agree with me on all points then and there, granted merely an understanding of my language. The witness would not be bound to agree that it was the dean, whom he or she might not know, nor expected to know anything about the check or a daughter in Belgium.

In short, an observation sentence is something that we can depend on other witnesses to agree to at the time of the event or situation described. A witness might of course forget and give divergent testimony later, or might fail to notice a feature at the time until it was pointed out. But the witness can check and assent if asked at the time. The reason for such agreement is that the terms used in an observation sentence are terms that we can all apply to their objects on sight: terms like "mailbox", "stout man", "gray moustache", "rimless spectacles", "Homburg hat",

"walking stick". They are terms unlike "dean of the law
school", "birthday", "daughter in Belgium"; for in applying these terms to the present situation we depend on past
experiences that few have been privileged to share.

"The cat is on the mat" qualifies as an observation sentence. "My cat is on the mat" does not, on our definition,
since another witness might not know whose cat it was.
Even our observation sentence may sometimes be truth-
fully uttered without reporting a present observation;
thus "The cat is on the mat" may sometimes express a
belief based on earlier observation or mere hearsay. In
calling it an observation sentence we mean that it is a
form of words that *can* be used to report a present event
or situation, and that other witnesses can then be counted
on to concur if queried at the time.

It is easy to see why some of our sentences are bound
to be of this kind, if we reflect on how we learn language.
Some terms, and short sentences containing them, are
learned in the sensible presence of something that the
term describes, or in the circumstances that the sentence
reports. This way of learning expressions is what philosophers call "ostensive." It is a simple matter of learning to
associate the heard words with things simultaneously observed—a matter, as modern psychologists put it, of conditioning. Thus, we may venture to volunteer or assent to
the word "yellow" in the presence of something yellow,
on hearing others do so. This way of responding will be
reinforced, as psychologists say, by social approval or successful communication, and so become habitual. The part
of language that we learn first must be learned ostensively, thus not depending on other language-learning.

Further vocabulary is acquired afterward by processes
that depend on prior acquisitions. Learning by ostension
depends on no prior acquisitions. By ostension we learn to
use and react to observation sentences.

Typical observation sentences are about bodies: "This is a table," "This table is square," "The cat is on the mat." Always the situation that makes an observation sentence true will be a situation that is intersubjectively observable; that is, it will be the sort of situation to which multiple witnesses could, if present, attest. Further, it will be a situation that the witnesses can witness one another's witnessing of. These crucial traits are assured by the distinctive nature of ostension. The learner of the language has to be able to observe the relevant situation simultaneously with hearing the veteran speaker affirm the sentence and must also be able to observe that the speaker's affirming of the sentence is accompanied by observations of that same situation. Correspondingly, the veteran speaker who ventures to judge the learner's performance has to be able to observe that the learner, when affirming the sentence, is observing the appropriate situation.

There are two traits of observation sentences which, when considered side by side, invite a philosophical question. The distinguishing feature of observation sentences is that they can be checked on the spot. Yet these sentences are commonly about enduring bodies—cats, mats, tables. How is this possible? That there are enduring bodies at all, behind the passing show of sensory appearance, is a point of physical theory—a rudimentary point, but still something beyond the observable present occasion. How then can a sentence about bodies be at the same time an observation sentence, for which the whole occasion for affirmation is the observable present?

This puzzle comes of viewing the matter from the wrong end. The special virtue of observation sentences is that we can in principle learn them by ostension as wholes, keyed as wholes to the appropriate observable occasions, before ever learning to link the component words to enduring bodies. "The cat is on the mat" can be

learned ostensively as a unitary string of syllables in association with a certain range of possible scenes. All of us
necessarily learned some observation sentences thus.
Then, as we gradually caught on to the theory of enduring
bodies, we came to treat some of the component words as
referring to bodies. Learning by ostension, as a trained
animal might, to associate whole observation sentences
with appropriate patterns of stimulation, is a first indispensable step toward learning physical theory. We get on
into the theory afterward, bit by bit, as we learn to dis-
member the observation sentences and make further use
of their component words. It is to this primary, ostensive
learning of observation sentences as wholes that physical
theory itself owes its vital continuing connection with
sensory evidence.

Probably none of us in fact learned "The cat is on the
mat" outright by ostension, but we could have. A likelier
example is "(This is a) ball," or "Yellow." An important
trait of language is that people learn it by different routes
and no record of the route is preserved in the words
learned. What makes a sentence an observation sentence
is not that it *was* learned ostensively but that it is of a sort
that *could* have been. And what sort is that? We already
said: it is a sentence whose whole occasion of affirmation,
nearly enough, is the intersubjectively observable present
occasion. This is a straightforward trait attaching to some
sentences and not others. And it is a trait that is socially
traceable, for what it comes to is just that all speakers of
the language, nearly enough, will assent to the sentence
under the same concurrent stimulations. "The table is
square" and "The cat is on the mat" will pass this test and
so qualify as observation sentences. "This is a bachelor"
will not qualify as an observation sentence, since one of
two tested speakers may happen to know that the man
pointed to is a bachelor while the other does not.

Ostension accounts for our acquisition of only a modest part of our language. A major source is an elaborate and largely unconscious process of abstraction and generalization, working partly from what we have previously learned by ostension and depending heavily on imitation of observed use. We guess the force of one sentence by noting its use in relation to other sentences; we grasp the use of a word by abstraction from sentences in which it turns up; and we learn how to build new sentences by copying the structure observed in old ones. There is much that could be said, and much more still to be learned, about these methods.

A less mysterious form that such derivative acquisition can take, though not the most frequent, is definition. The simplest form of definition, in turn, is that in which the new expression is equated outright to some expression that is presumed to have been already intelligible. Thus, if we suppose the words "parent", "brother", "married", and "man" already to have been somehow acquired, we might explain "uncle" and "bachelor" by equating them to "parent's brother" and "unmarried man". Other definitions are contextual; in these the new expression is not equated to anything outright, but systematic instructions are given for translating all desired sentences containing the expression. For instance, we might define "brother", not by formulating any direct substitute for the word by itself, but by systematically explaining all sentences in which the word occurs followed by "of". This we could do by translating "brother of x" as "male other than x whose parents are the parents of x." Or again we might define the connective "if and only if", not outright, but by systematically explaining all the compound sentences that are obtained by putting "if and only if" between sentences. We simply explain "p if and only if q" as "if p then q and if q then p."

Observation sentences are the bottom edge of language, where it touches experience: where speech is conditioned to stimulation. It is ultimately through them that language in general gains its meaning, its bearing on reality. This is why it is they that convey the basic evidence for all belief, all scientific theory. They play this fundamental role not only when someone is checking over his or her beliefs after a prediction has gone wrong, but equally when someone is marshaling evidence for a belief that has been challenged by a colleague. And it is here that the social trait just now attributed to observation sentences is crucial—that all speakers assent to such a sentence under the same stimulations. As dissident theorists converge toward observation sentences they converge to agreement.

An observation may be made by an individual; but, as we have emphasized, the truth of the observation sentence is an intersubjective matter. Here a favorite old irrationalist doctrine finds both its seductiveness and its rebuttal. The hoary view contends that truth is relative to believer; there's truth for me and truth for you, and their reconciliation is generally neither possible nor desirable. Now the variable ownership of acts of observation might be cited in support of this doctrine. For haven't we said that observations are the ultimate basis for belief systems? And can't we be expected, you and I, to make different observations? Maybe so; but which observation sentences are *true* will not thus depend on either of us, nor on any other observer. The firmness of our respective grounds for accepting a given observation sentence may vary, and so may our appraisal of that sentence; but its truth cannot. Happily, we need not acquiesce in the ultimacy of disagreement in order to appreciate its sources. Intersubjective conflict, to be sure, is unlike intrasubjective conflict in one important way: the former, but not the latter, may be recognized as such without thereby gaining impetus for giving way. But where your beliefs and mine are mutually inconsistent we cannot both be right, any more than I alone can be right in each of several incompatible beliefs.

So we all contribute, with our respective observations, to the knowledge that we all share. We find here an element that at once makes science hard and makes it possible. It is hard because it must build a coherent system from the diverse evidence gleaned and reported by people of different times, places, cultures, and interests; it is possible because there is thus so much to draw on.

Are observation sentences infallible? Nearly, if we set aside those offered disingenuously and those uttered by speakers who have not quite learned the language. It would strain the very meaning of the words, in such sentences, to suppose any appreciable fallibility; for the words are themselves acquired through the association of observation sentences with the observable circumstances of their utterance.

A trace of fallibility, indeed, there is. Normally, observation is the tug that tows the ship of theory; but in an extreme case the theory pulls so hard that observation yields. It can happen that a theory has long gone unchallenged, neatly conforming to countless relevant observations on every hand, and that now one observation conflicts with it. Chances are that we will waive the one wayward observation. This still does not mean going back on our definition of an observation sentence. We defined it as a sentence to which all witnesses are bound to accede at the time of the observed event; we left them free to change their minds afterward. In the cases where we waive an observation—and they had better be pretty special—we are changing our minds after the occasion, or, more usually, doubting someone else's report.

It is never a matter of rejecting an observation sentence on the occasion of the observation. And an observation sentence ceases to be an observation sentence, after all, when we change the tense of its verb. Reports of past observations involve inference, as lately remarked. It is only these, and not strictly observation sentences, that we are second-guessing when we waive the wayward observation.

Despite any such legalisms, however, our memories are not to be lightly dismissed, much less our records. Nor are the reports of observation by trusted colleagues, though the trust in this quarter admits of degrees. It is only a strong and long unchallenged theory that will occasionally resist the adverse testimony of a remembered or recorded or reported observation. In such an extremity we may attribute the wayward evidence to unexplained interference, even to hallucination. If such alleged cases of hallucination tend to cluster in a few persons, who may then be seen as prone to hallucination, so much the better for our scientific conscience. There is then hope of accommodating the very waywardness of those wayward observations in a theory too, a theory of psychopathology. Law may thus be sought in the apparent breaches of law.

Even when observations persist in conflicting with a theory, the theory will not necessarily be abandoned forthwith. It will linger until a plausible substitute is found; the conflicting observations will stand unexplained, and the sense of crisis will mount.

> Galileo's contributions to the study of motion depended closely upon difficulties discovered in Aristotle's theory by scholastic critics. Newton's new theory of light and color originated in the discovery that none of the existing ... theories would account for the length of the spectrum, and the wave theory that replaced Newton's was announced in

the midst of growing concern about anomalies in the relation of diffraction and polarization effects to Newton's theory. Thermodynamics was born from the collision of two
existing nineteenth-century physical theories, and quantum mechanics from a variety of difficulties surrounding
black-body radiation, specific heats, and the photoelectric
effect. Furthermore, in all these cases except that of Newton the awareness of anomaly had lasted so long and pene-
trated so deep that one can appropriately describe the fields
affected by it as in a state of growing crisis. Because it
demands ... major shifts in the problems and techniques
of normal science, the emergence of new theories is generally preceded by a period of pronounced professional insecurity. As one might expect, that insecurity is generated
by the persistent failure of the puzzles of normal science
to come out as they should. Failure of existing rules is the
prelude to a search for new ones.[1]

There are some points at which, without deliberate consideration of theories, all of us find it second nature to edit
observation. We learn to take it that sticks appearing bent
while partially immersed in water should in fact be
judged straight. We learn not to suppose that the moon is
larger when near the horizon than when higher in the
sky. When the colors before us begin to vibrate, we do not
imagine that the properties of light have changed. But in
all these examples, again, we are at pains in the end to
accommodate the waywardness of the observations in a
theory too. The illusion of the immersed sticks is covered
by a physical theory of refraction; the illusion of the low
moon is coped with by some psychological hypotheses;
and a general visual disruption is apt to set us speculating
about something we ate or drank. Observations thus stub-

---

[1] T. S. Kuhn, *The Structure of Scientific Revolutions* (Chicago and London: The University of Chicago, 1962), pp. 67f.

bornly retain their primacy. They remain the boundary conditions of our body of beliefs.

It must be confessed however that not all observations, or reports of observations, are so conscientiously accommodated. Some of them, uncongenial to existing theory, get passed over with even less acknowledgment than it would take to rate them as hallucinations. Persistent reports of occult experiences receive this short treatment, as also, of late, many of the reports of unidentified flying objects. Note, however, that a good scientist does not treat an uncongenial observation in this high-handed way when the observation is induced by an experiment of his own. For his experiment will have been designed for the very purpose of deciding between two alternative moves in the development of his theory, two preconceived alternative beliefs. But he will perhaps dismiss a puzzling observation, reported to him with palpable sincerity or even made by himself, if he has in mind no specific change of theory that might accommodate the observation and still jibe with previous data. Up to a point this high-handedness is justifiable. If a scientist were to interrupt existing projects in order to find a plausible hypothesis for every puzzling experience outside the laboratory, and if he were to lend a patient and judicious ear to every crank and gossip, he would learn less.

Scientists are so good nowadays at discovering truth that it is trivial to condone their methods and absurd to criticize them. At the same time it is evident that waiving observations is always a delicate business. A theory that is sustained only at the cost of systematic waiving is an undependable instrument of prediction and not a good example of scientific method.

Just because it is not feasible to accommodate all observations all the time, some philosophers have wanted to scout the whole idea of observation. Their doubts have been aggravated by a further consideration: the air of subjectivity that seems to them to render the very idea of observation hopelessly vague. Where the untrained eye observes a wired metal box, the trained eye observes a condenser. Where the untrained eye observes nothing, the trained eye observes the recent trace of a deer. But again these discrepancies are no ground for misgivings when properly viewed; they are only a play on the careless use of a word.

For philosophical purposes the notion of observation, and of observation sentence, needs to be taken with an unimaginative literalness. A straightforward criterion to the purpose is already before us: that all reasonably competent speakers of the language be disposed, if asked, to assent to the sentence under the same stimulations of their sensory surfaces. On this criterion "That's a condenser" simply does not count as an observation sentence, trained eye notwithstanding. Naturally the experts, being reasonable, will stop pressing for further evidence anyway as soon as they can agree. They can agree that it is a condenser, so they stop there, rather than press on compulsively to genuine observation sentences in our sense of the term; but they always could press on. If they care to use the term "observation" for their intermediate stopping point, let us not dispute about the term. They might be said to be simply narrowing the category of "competent speakers of the language" to their specialized group.

We remarked that some philosophers have identified observations with events of sensation. It is thus not to be wondered that in some philosophical writings the title of observation sentence is reserved for sentences very different from observation sentences as we have defined them. It is reserved for introspective reports like "I am in pain" and "I seem to see blue now." Such reports also have been rated as infallible. It must be conceded that they tend to be incontestable, because of the speaker's privileged access to his or her private experience. But on this very point they differ diametrically from observation sentences in our sense. The situations that make them true are not ones to which multiple witnesses could attest. What is open to public observation in such a case is rather the introspective report itself. What is comparable to the cat's being on the mat is not the person's feeling pain or seeing blue, but the reporting pain or blue—the verbal behavior. This verbal behavior is indeed available as a datum for further theorizing; it is a datum to which multiple witnesses might attest.

Chapter IV

Self-Evidence

We noted an important class of beliefs that do not rest on other beliefs. Those were the beliefs expressed by observation sentences. Now there is also another class of beliefs of which the same can be said: beliefs that are *self-evident*, that go without saying. It goes without saying that water is wet, that oculists treat eyes, that puppies are young, that no bachelor is married, that every brother has a brother or sister, that the parts of parts of a thing are parts of the thing. What distinguishes these beliefs is that they look for support neither to other beliefs nor to observation. To understand them is to hold them. There are also beliefs which, though they would never be questioned, seem not to deserve the title of self-evidence; for example, that there have been dogs. The title of self-evidence would seem odd here mainly because *other* evidence is so evident, namely our observations of dogs.

To what do the self-evident ones owe their truth? To the meanings of the words, we may be told. "Bachelor" means "unmarried man"; "puppy" means "young dog"; "oculist" means "eye doctor". In defense of this doctrine it might be said that if anyone were seriously to deny that oculists treat eyes, or the other examples, he would be giving odd meanings to the words. But this defense is more apparent than real. If on a cold day a man seriously remarks how warm it is, we have good reason to suppose he misunderstands a word. Perhaps he has associated "cold" with his native *caldo,* and hence "warm" with *freddo.* Yet it does not follow that "It is cold" is true simply because of the meanings of its words and independently of the weather. The simple fact is that whenever anyone denies a sentence which, in the circumstances or in general, is obviously true, we have evidence that he has missed a meaning. In particular, then, nothing has really been said to show that "Water is wet," "Oculists treat eyes," and the rest are true *due* to meaning—nothing beyond calling them self-evident, which is where we came in.

All truths depend on meanings at least in part, of course; for, by supplanting a word by some other that differs in meaning, we can make any true sentence false. Of a sentence that is obviously true and depends in no obvious way on observations or prior beliefs, one might then say that its truth is based solely on meanings—just because there is no other basis to point to. If this is the doctrine, well and good—so long as we do not take it to be telling us anything.

Among the self-evident truths there are some that are called *logically true:* thus "Every horse that is white is a horse." This particular truth illustrates a general logical principle: "Every *A* that is *B* is an *A.*" Our instance comes from the general principle by substitution: "horse" for *"A"* and "white" for *"B".* As support of the particular case, however, the general principle is superfluous; for it cannot be more obviously true than its instance, which affirms so

much less. Anyway, to adduce support to "Every horse
that is white is a horse" would be to adduce coals to New-
castle.

Some philosophers claim that logical truths are true
because of the meanings of the basic little logical words
—in this case "every", "that", "is", and "an". Again it is not
clear that this account really adds anything.

Thus far we have seen only an example of logical truth.
Which truths, altogether, count as logical truths? A way
of demarcating them from the rest of the truths is suggested by the schematism that we used in "Every *A* that
is *B* is an *A*." Here is a formula built of what we may call
logical particles—"every", "that", "is", and "an"—along
with letters as blanks, substitution for which gives the
formula's instances. This is a formula, or form, all of
whose instances are true sentences, indeed logical truths.
The suggestion is that in general we call a sentence logically true when it is an instance of some form built of just
logical particles and blanks, and all instances of that form
are true.

The form may be called a *logical form*, meaning that
besides blanks it contains just logical particles. Further, it
may be called *valid*, meaning that all its instances are
true. So the suggestion is that we call a sentence *logically
true* when it is an instance of a valid logical form. Thus
"Every horse that is white is a horse" counts as logically
true because it is an instance of the valid logical form
"Every *A* that is *B* is an *A*."

Our definition of logical truth, that is, of which truths
to count as logical, depends thus on a notion of logical
form, which depends in turn on some enumeration of the
logical particles. We noted "every", "that", "is", and "an";
others are "and", "or", "not", "if", "but", "some". Care must
be taken, however, not to abuse the logical forms. "Every
A that is *B* is an *A*" may be all very well, but its variant

"Every *BA* is an *A*," as in "Every white horse is a horse,"
skirts pitfalls. What are we to say of "Every expectant
mother is a mother," or "Every intellectual dwarf is a
dwarf"? In view of such examples, and for the sake in
general of a streamlined theory and an efficient technique,
it is customary in logic to paraphrase the logical forms
into a more systematic and economical notation, mathematical in spirit. We shall not need, however, to broach
that apparatus here.

Self-evidence, whatever its cause, is the conspicuous
trait of "Every horse that is white is a horse." It cannot be
said to be a trait of all logical truths, but there is a derivative trait that can. When a logical truth is too complicated
to be appreciated out of hand, it can be proved from self-
evident truths by a series of steps each of which is itself
self-evident—in a word, it can be *deduced* from them.
This trait is *demonstrability*. It may be called *absolute*
demonstrability when there is need to distinguish it from
the *relative* case where something is deducible only from
some previously established or accepted beliefs or stated
hypotheses which are not themselves self-evident. Even
the absolutely demonstrable truths will outrun the logical
ones, since self-evidence is not confined to the logical
truths.

The trait of self-evidence is not hard and fast. Some
truths may be self-evident for one person and in need of
proof for another person. An example, perhaps, is the logical truth:

> If you help none who help themselves, you do not help
> yourself.

If we have a friend who does not find the truth of this
sentence self-evident, we might try to prove the sentence
to him by deriving it from one or more sentences that are

self-evident to him, by steps which are self-evident to
him. For instance, giving our friend no great credit, we
might start with the self-evident truth:

> In helping yourself, you help at least one self-helper
> (namely yourself).

From this it self-evidently follows that:

> If you do not help at least one self-helper, you do not help
> yourself

and thence that:

> If you help none who help themselves, you do not help
> yourself

which was to be proved.

We see from this example how even a brief logical truth
may fail to be self-evident, but still be absolutely demonstrable. It is an important fact that absolutely demonstrable truths may fall so far short of being self-evident as to
be extraordinarily difficult to see or even counter-intuitive. As we observe from the uses of computers, the linking of large numbers of trivial little steps may yield
knowledge that is itself neither trivial nor obvious.

The category of logical truths owes its importance
mainly to the derivative notion of logical implication.
This notion can be defined in terms of logical truth as
follows: one sentence logically implies another when the
compound sentence which we get by combining the two
in the fashion "If p then q" is logically true. For instance,
the sentence "The world was without form and void" logically implies the sentence "The world was void"; and to
say that it does so is simply to attribute logical truth to the

sentence "If the world was without form and void then the world was void." Similarly our logical truth about self help affords a logical implication: "You help none who help themselves" logically implies "You do not help yourself." Logical implication is also called logical consequence or deducibility, but in reverse order: "You do not help yourself" is a logical consequence of, or logically deducible from, "You help none who help themselves." Logical implication is the relation which relates any theory or hypothesis to its logical consequences.

The term "implication", and its alternatives "consequence" and "deducible", have also a broader and vaguer application without the qualifier "logical". One sentence is said to imply another whenever, starting with the one sentence plus perhaps some self-evident truths, you can get to the other sentence by a series of self-evident steps. This broad notion of implication or consequence or deducibility is useful and widely used, but vague insofar as we have not settled just what to count as self-evident. Logical implication is the well-defined core of implication, and the techniques governing it are the central business of logic.

The importance of implication is that it transmits truth. A falsehood will imply both truths and falsehoods, but a truth implies only truths.

Besides the simple case where one sentence implies another, there is also joint implication, where several sentences join forces to do the implying. There was an example of this in the murder mystery of Chapter I, where (1), (2), and (3) taken together implied that Cabot committed the crime. A sentence is bound to be true if it is implied jointly by several sentences all of which are true. The joint case is readily turned into a simple case, since we have only to join the implying sentences to one another with help of the logical particle "and" to form a single sentence.

<u>Implication is what makes our system of beliefs cohere.</u>
If we see that a sentence is implied by sentences that we
believe true, we are obliged to believe it true as well, or
else change our minds about one or another of the sentences that jointly implied it. If we see that the negation
of some sentence is implied by sentences that we believe
true, we are obliged to disbelieve that sentence or else
change our minds about one of the others. Implication is
thus the very texture of our web of belief, and logic is the
theory that traces it.

Logical implication consists, we saw, in the logical
truth of a *conditional:* of a sentence of the form "If *p* then
q." Hence, we suggested, the importance of logical truth.
As for the logical truths, they can all be proved, it was
said, by self-evident steps from self-evident truths. Logical theory proceeds more efficiently, however, by ad-
dressing itself to valid logical forms rather than to the
logically true sentences that are their instances. It is here
that the logical forms are principally useful, for they de-
pict features relevant to logical truth, suppressing irrele-
vancies. The forms "Every *A* that is *B* is an *A*" and
"Whoever *R*s none who *R* themselves does not *R* himself"[1] take all sentences of those forms in their stride once
for all, so that there is no cause to pause in particular over
white horses or persons who help themselves.

Instead of just specifying that the beginnings are to be
self-evident, the logician is apt to specify some valid log-

---

[1]Or, if we prefer to be more pedantic about logical particles, we might
say rather that "whoever" and "who" and "him" are not pure logical
particles, because they involve the notion of person, which belongs
rather to anthropology than to logic. Then we would paraphrase "whoever" in our example as "whatever person", and "none" as "no person",
and "who" as "which", and "himself" as "itself", and thus isolate the valid
logical form "Whatever *A R*s no *A* which *R*s itself does not *R* itself."
Here *"A"* is a blank for any common noun such as "person", and *"R"* is
a blank for any transitive verb such as "help", and the other words are
incontestably logical particles.

ical forms as his explicit starting point. These he calls
axioms. Likewise, instead of just leaving any further valid
logical forms to be derived from the axioms by self-evident steps, he specifies certain allowable steps, or *rules of
inference.* For instance, he might start with axioms including, among a half dozen others, the valid logical form
"p or not *p"* (using *"p"* to stand for sentences). One of his
rules of inference might be this: from *"p* or *q"* infer *"q* or
p." Applying this rule to the axiom *"p* or not *p,"* he gets
as a theorem the new valid logical form "not *p* or *p."* From
this in turn, by some other of his rules, he gets a second
theorem. From a small but judicious choice of axioms and
rules of inference (less trivial on the average than the
present examples), every valid logical form can be generated as a theorem. This important fact was established
only in 1928–30 by work of Skolem and Gödel.

Complete coverage of logical truth can be managed
equally by each of many alternative sets of axioms and
rules of inference. Formal proof procedures are also available which follow other patterns than that of axioms and
rules of inference. We will not elaborate on the various
alternatives here; let us just say what all formal proof
procedures have in common. The keynote is susceptibility
to routine check by inspection of formulas. We can tell on
inspection whether a proposed sentence falls under one of
the axioms, and we can tell on inspection whether a
proposed step falls under one of the rules of inference. If
a proof procedure departs from the axiom and rule pattern,
still its applications must be similarly susceptible to
check. Otherwise we do not call it a proof procedure.

The development of formal proof procedures was necessary for a deep understanding of logic—the kind of understanding reflected in the theorem of Skolem and Godel,
among others. That development must not, however, be
allowed to obscure the part that is played, now as before,

by self-evidence. However formal a proof procedure may be, the trustworthiness of the theorems that it generates still depends ultimately upon our conviction that each of the axioms is logically valid and our conviction that none of the rules of inference can lead from a form that is valid to a form that is not.

Speaking of proof reminds us of mathematics, where proof is so much the pattern. May we not say of mathematical truths generally what we have said of logical truths, that all are demonstrable? This would mean that each truth of mathematics was either self-evident or derivable from self-evident truths by self-evident steps—and such was once the general belief. However, difficulties arise. They are best illustrated in the area known as set theory.

Sets, or classes, are basic for mathematics; many of the fundamental portions of mathematics seem to require the notion of set for their systematic development. It is a curiously versatile notion, overwhelmingly productive. Sets do more than serve as auxiliaries to various branches of mathematics; they are capable even of simulating numbers themselves, and functions, and all the other objects, of pure mathematics, so that the whole of mathematics can be systematically reinterpreted as having to do exclusively with sets. But this universe of sets is no meager universe; it must be taken to comprise not only sets of individuals but sets of sets, sets of sets of sets, and so on up.

These sets, or classes, are objects determined by their members, that is, by the objects that belong to them. So to specify just which members a set has is to specify the set. Now specification of members need not proceed by a simple listing of them; obviously such listing cannot be achieved for sets with infinitely many members. So we often specify a set's membership, and therewith the set itself, by citing some condition that is both necessary and sufficient for membership in that set. Thus, we might specify the set of even integers by citing the condition of being the double of an integer; this condition is met by all and only the members of the set. It is natural to suppose that whenever we give such a condition we succeed in specifying a set—the set whose members are exactly the objects that meet the condition. Once accustomed to speaking of sets in this way, one might indeed suppose it self-evident that there is a set for each condition citable. Brilliant mathematicians did once suppose this. Yet it cannot be true.

For consider the condition of *not* being a set that is a member of itself. This is the condition, in short, of non-self-membership. Almost any object that comes to mind fulfills this condition; for example, the set of even integers, not being itself the double of an integer, surely fulfills it. But there is nonetheless no set whose members are exactly the objects meeting the condition of non-self-membership. For suppose there were a set of just those objects. Let us call the alleged set x. Just the things that are not members of themselves are members of x. But then, in particular, if x is not a member of itself, it qualifies as a member of x—hence of itself, involving us in a contradiction. If on the other hand x *is* a member of itself, then by the condition for membership it does not belong in x, so we are again in contradiction. We have to conclude that there is no such set x after all. *Nothing has as members all and only what does not have itself as member.* This is even a logical truth. Its logical form, "Nothing Rs all and only what does not R itself," is a valid logical form.

The sentence italicized above illustrates that even a fairly brief logical truth can be not merely unobvious but, indeed, counter-intuitive. Named for its discoverer, it is known as Russell's paradox. It is the simplest of the many paradoxes of set theory. It is a paradox of set theory though a logical truth. What is paradoxical about it is that it runs against a set-theoretic expectation—the expectation that there be a set for each expressible membership condition.

One lesson of these paradoxes is that self-evidence is not to be attributed lightly. Another is that the truths of set theory, or the sentences of set theory that are to be regarded as truths, cannot be expected to be absolutely demonstrable (as logical truths were); that is, derivable from self-evident truths by self-evident steps. What one now does in set theory is adopt special axioms of set existence, not as self-evident truths but as hypotheses comparable to the hypotheses of theoretical physics. One then deduces consequences, by steps of inference which are themselves of course still self-evident. One examines the consequences and then perhaps tinkers with the axioms some more, much as one might with hypotheses in physics, to see if a neater system can be devised to the same practical purposes.

Another principle long taken by mathematicians to be self-evident was the Euclidean parallels postulate, which asserts that there is exactly one parallel to a given line through any point off that line. The parallels postulate has been shown not to be deducible from the other Euclidean postulates. On the contrary, it is replaceable by any of various contrary postulates without loss of systematic consistency. And far from being requisite for our physics, the parallels postulate has even been supplanted there by one of those variants.

Not all mathematics has lost touch with self-evidence to this degree. A much better behaved part is elementary number theory, which is roughly the arithmetic and algebra of the positive integers. Here there are no known paradoxes—no propositions that seem self-evident and prove false. Better behaved though it be, however, elementary number theory presents some easily formulable questions that have resisted definitive answer for centuries.

Here there is a situation very unlike what one finds in the logical truths. Godel has shown that no formal proof procedure for elementary number theory can be complete. No proof procedure can be so strong that all the truths of elementary number theory (and no falsehoods) admit of proof under it. Every proof procedure must miss some truths of elementary number theory or let in some falsehoods. In the light of Godel's result it is quite implausible that all truths of elementary number theory are, like the logical truths, absolutely demonstrable in our sense: derivable from self-evident truths by self-evident steps. Inasmuch as number theory is embedded in set theory, Godel's result has this consequence for set theory *a fortiori.*

Thus, it seems that mathematics generally (including geometry and number theory as well as set theory) is from an evidential point of view more like physics and less like logic than was once supposed. On the whole the truths of mathematics can be deduced not from self-evident axioms, but only from hypotheses which, like those of natural science, are to be judged by the plausibility of their consequences.

Other kinds of claims have also been held self-evident. There are the claims vaguely known as *limiting principles:* principles, broadly philosophical in tone, that disallow one or another general sort of scientific hypothesis. One such is the principle that nothing can come out of nothing, better known by its venerable Latin equivalent *Ex nihilo nihil fit.* This purports to tell us not what there is in the universe, but that, whatever there is, each thing was either always there or sprang from something else.

Now what is remarkable about this principle is that it has lately had a narrow escape from repudiation, a curious indignity for an allegedly self-evident principle to have to suffer. For there has been in recent years a staunchly supported, if bizarre, cosmological theory called the *steady-state* theory. It holds that hydrogen atoms are continually coming into existence without coming from anything at all. This, the theory goes, is how we are to explain the observed density of the universe. We know empirically that each galaxy is rapidly receding from all others. If we assume what has been called the "perfect cosmological principle"—that the general state of the universe is roughly uniform through time as well as space—then, were there not "continuous creation," the density of the universe would by now be much less than it is found to be. Although the steady-state theory sounds implausible, it was defended by some reputable astronomers as the solution to a paradox.

The steady-state theory was put forward as a rival to another cosmological theory, which had taught rather that in the beginning there was a cosmic explosion whence the recession of the galaxies began. We can represent this rivalry as a conflict of two limiting principles; the steady-state theory sustains the perfect cosmological principle at the cost of sacrificing the *Ex nihilo nihil,* while the explosion theory does the opposite. It happens that the steady-state theory has after all been losing out to the explosion theory, because of discoveries about the age of galaxies. So we learn here that limiting principles are not in general self-evident, being capable of conflicting. And we learn also that principles with even one foot in physics are answerable to empirical findings.

Another limiting principle to view warily is "Every event has a cause." As a philosopher's maxim it may seem safe enough if the philosopher is willing to guide it

around recalcitrant facts. But this principle, in the face of
quantum theory, needs extensive guiding. Physicists tell
us that individual electrons and other elementary particles do not conform in their behavior to rigidly determi-
nate laws. A radioactive substance emits its particles at
random; it is impossible not only in practice but in principle to say just which of its particles will be the next to
depart, or just when. The principle that every event has
a cause can still be retained, like other limiting principles,
if one is willing to make enough sacrifices for it. But
insofar as it purports to be a principle of physics, it cannot
be counted as self-evident even if it somehow survives
modern quantum theory.

When the scientist has to think up some change or other
in the structure of his theory in order to accommodate an
unexpected observation, the limiting principles afford a
helpful guide by narrowing his choices and encouraging
continuity with tradition. An extreme situation can arise,
however, where conformity to all the limiting principles
would require excessive artificiality or complexity of theory; and in such a crisis, as we have seen, one or another
limiting principle may give way. On the whole, thus,
such principles measure up poorly to standards of self-
evidence. Logic and mathematics seem to be the only domains where self-evidence manages to rise above
triviality; and this it does, in those domains, by a linking
of self-evidence on to self-evidence in the chain reaction
known as proof. And even mathematics lends itself only
partially to such treatment; this was brought home to us
by Russell's paradox, Euclid's postulate of parallels, and
Godel's incompleteness theorem.

Self-evidence is sometimes ascribed to judgments of
moral value. Instances of such ascription in the Declaration of Independence come to mind; but surely those com-
mendable sentiments have been less universally shared,

early and late, than self-evidence would require. A moral precept that perhaps has more of a claim to self-evidence is "One should not inflict needless pain." Mostly, however, what the ascription of self-evidence to a moral precept is apt to reflect is just a resolution that the precept is to be regarded as basic and hence as exempt from discussion. We resolve to treat such a maxim as a starting point rather than as standing in need of support itself. But even here, should several principles be advanced, questions of their consistency might very well arise. For add "One should not tell lies" to "One should not inflict needless pain"; these two mild injunctions can combine to create practical dilemmas in imaginable cases.

Chapter V

Testimony

Two basic ways in which language serves us are these: as a means of getting others to do what we want them to, and as a means of learning from others what we want to know. In the one way it affords us, vicariously, more hands to work with; in the other, more eyes to see with. It is to our interest to predict what will happen, and what would happen if we did one thing or another. Observation is a vital ingredient in all such prediction, and our chances of prediction are much increased by increased observation. So in its yield of vicarious observation, through the testimony of others, language confers a major benefit.

This testimonial or information-gathering function of language has as its primitive vehicle the observation sentence. This, we saw in Chapter II, is the part of language that everyone acquires or can acquire by ostension; in other words, by a direct conditioning of sentences to the relevant stimulations. So when we hear an observation sentence that reports something beyond our own experience, we gain evidence that the speaker has the stimulation appropriate for its utterance, even though that stimulation does not reach us. Such, in principle, is the mechanism of testimony as an extension of our senses. It was the first and greatest human device for stepping up the observational intake. Telescopes, microscopes, radar, and radio-astronomy are later devices to the same end.

In speaking of enlarged or vicarious observation, we speak figuratively. Literally speaking a record even of our own past observations is an object of present observation and only causally connected with the observations that it records. Similarly, in the case of the instruments, it is only the lens image or the microphotograph or the radar blip that is literally the object of observation. The object thereby revealed, the dark star or the protein molecule or whatever, is of course literally an unobserved object with which our observations are only causally connected. Similarly, in the case of another man's observation report, our observation in the literal sense is limited to the sound of his words—words with which *his* reported observations are causally connected. Especially in this last case, we in practice make the causal leap without a moment's reflection, because of the social nature of our very learning of the primitive vocabulary of observation. We learned this vocabulary in the first place by linking the sound of another's words to observations shared at the time of their utterance.

Observation sentences, taken narrowly, are comparatively foolproof. That is what makes them the tribunal of science. It is when we move to other sentences that the danger of mistaken testimony soars. On the other hand neither the observation sentences nor the others are knaveproof. What about lies?

It would be a sorry world if we could not usually trust
our fellow man. The great and ancient value of testimony
as an extension of our senses would be gone if there were
not a reasonably high correlation between testimony and
truth. A high negative correlation would serve. If we
could count on people to lie most of the time, we could get
all the information from their testimony that we get under the present system. We could even construe all their
statements as containing an understood and unspoken
"not", and hence as predominantly true after all. Utterly
random veracity, however, meshed with random men-
dacity, would render language useless for gathering information.

Since no one would like that, it may appear that it behooves no one to lie. This reasoning, however, unfortu-
nately for all of us, is erroneous. A melancholy truth of
moral philosophy is involved here which applies not only
to lying. The melancholy general point is that what a man
gains from the law-abiding behavior of his fellows can be
further augmented by his own violations. Take the case of
a burning theater. A man's chance of escape is best if he
bolts for the door and others file out in orderly fashion.
His chances are poor if everyone bolts for the door. However, his own bolting will not itself cause others to bolt,
not soon enough or in sufficient numbers to destroy his
advantage. Similar remarks apply to all sorts of cheating.
This is dangerous information, and the reader may take it
as a compliment that we have ventured to share it with
him. Anyway the fat was already in the fire. This is why
society establishes legal penalties against theft and various other forms of cheating. The penalties offset the private advantage.

There is no general law against lying. Yet there is a
marked tendency for people to tell the truth, as they see
it, at least when they see nothing to gain by lying. Perhaps

we can account for this happy tendency in terms of the very mechanisms that make for the learning of language itself. Our learning of the primitive vocabulary of observation sentences consists, after all, in our learning to associate it with the appropriate sensory stimulations. Small wonder then if those same stimulations dispose us in future to affirm the properly associated observation sentences. Lying is an effortful deviation from the conditioned response. We have here made the point only for observation sentences, but something similar would seem to apply also to the obscurer and more complicated processes that go into the learning of higher parts of language.

If a force for veracity can thus be found in the very mechanism of language learning, a force for credulity can be found there equally. We learn to use expressions in the circumstances in which we find them used by others. In effect, therefore, we proceed on the implicit assumption that people were using the expressions fittingly and not in lies. It is an interesting question, even, how we ever attain to the temerity of viewing someone's statement as false. Why do we not always continue as learners of language and so accept each statement, together with its circumstances of utterance, as just that much further evidence of how the words are used? In answer to this philosophical question we might say that the turning point depends partly on how complex a language we will accept. Instead of construing special occurrences of certain words in special ways in order to count a man's statement true, we find it simpler after a point to count it false. In so doing we are apt to be guided also, however unconsciously, by hypotheses regarding plausible processes. By what processes, we may unconsciously ask ourselves, would that speaker himself ever have learned a language that was complicated in those ways? And by what more plausible pro-

cesses might he have been caused to utter an intentional
or inadvertent falsehood in this instance?

If we are given wrong directions in a foreign city, we
may conclude either that our informant was disoriented
or that we were mistaken about the native word for
"west". If we already have some facility in the language,
we may reasonably guess that he was disoriented; for this
is a common enough failing. On the other hand an anec-
dote that an eminent scholar tells about himself affords an
example of the opposite kind. He came to Prague, having
meanwhile learned serviceable Polish but less Czech.
Conversation at a social gathering ran to questions as to
the fate or whereabouts of various other scholars or mutual acquaintances who would likewise have been fleeing
the revolution. Our learned friend was happy to be able to
say, in answer to each of a succession of these questions,
"He is now in the West." He said it in Czech, using the
Czech form of the Polish *zachod,* "west". The company
was increasingly bewildered, for the Czech word means
"lavatory". The bewilderment settled into amusement.
They sensed that our friend was speaking the truth, but
speaking a twisted language. A process whereby he might
have mislearned the Czech word was more plausible than
any process whereby he might have come to believe, or
come to hope to make others believe, that all those ref-
ugees were in the lavatory.

Our recent reflections have given us cause to expect a
built-in tendency toward veracity on the part of speakers
and toward credulity on the part of listeners. Such tenden-
cies are indeed the rule, and a harmonious pair of tenden-
cies they are. However, it behooves us to watch the second
tendency critically in ourselves. Veracity is generally admirable, if not always prudent; but credulity, in more
than modest measure, is neither admirable nor prudent.
In general, the way to keep our credulity within proper

bounds is to continue to think, but consciously now, of plausible processes. It is on this score that observation sentences stand forth as fairly foolproof; whether to believe them hinges on questions of the speaker's morals and motives. But even the remembrance of a past observation, we noted, is not itself an observation; and the connection of most sentences with observation sentences is much more remote. Such remoteness brings with it all the opportunities for error with which we are so familiar. Thus, when assessing testimony other than pure observation reports we must keep this increasing danger in mind and take into consideration what opportunities the speaker may plausibly have had for gathering evidence for his or her claim. Such consideration of plausible process is needed, in these cases, in addition to questions of the speaker's morals and motives. Considerations of the one kind and the other give us reason to prefer the testimony of reference books to a neighbor's hearsay, and both to the claims of advertisers.

In courts of law the testimony of witnesses is customarily judged in part on how much of what they say appears to be favorable to them. It is easier to believe the man who tells us something he would appear to prefer concealed than the one whose testimony proclaims his own excellence or innocence. The assessing of courtroom testimony draws heavily on what one understands about human psychology and behavior under stress. The attorney who cross-examines must be able to sense what portions of the testimony might prove vulnerable. She must call together all that she believes about the case and the witness, all that she has learned about cross-examination from her own experience and study, then decide how to proceed. The courtroom is worthy of the attention of those who are inclined toward taking too much of what they are told at face value. It teaches a stern lesson. People disguise

the truth in certain situations, whether out of devious-
ness, self-deception, ignorance, or fear. They also, of
course, misremember, misjudge, and misreason.

It can be useful to form the habit of filing in one's memory, as it were, the sources of one's information. For it can
happen that sources once trusted will lose their authority
for us, and one would then like to know which beliefs
might merit reassessment. We may come to mistrust a
source on moral grounds, having found signs of private
interests and corruption, and we may also come to mistrust a source on methodological grounds, having found
signs of hasty thinking and poor access to data.

Say you believe that Millard Fillmore, the thirteenth
President of the United States, was born on January 7,
1800. Why do you believe this? You might say that you
remember hearing it in a lecture, or that you looked it up
in an encyclopedia—or even that its inclusion as an example in this paragraph is your ground. But of the last you
should be cautious. We might be giving an example of
mistaken belief. In fact we are not; if you wish, you may
now pause to verify that the cited date is correct.

Now did that convince you? If so, you trust us as author-
ities, at least on this. The invitation to look it up for yourself may have increased your confidence in the claim.
Beware of such devices; a writer or speaker can expect not
to be taken up on an invitation like this, so he gains by its
apparent forthrightness while risking little. If a speaker
ordered "Believe it because I tell you to," you might have
answered his arrogance with skepticism. The point is that
whether or not you accept the claim made by someone
else depends on how much you trust that person on the
matter.

An author of this book remarked after walking about
the principality of Monaco, "Just think—only eight square
miles!" "I don't see how you even get eight out of it," his

brother replied. The map was conclusive: you couldn't. Yet the Encyclopedia Britannica, the World Almanac, Scott's stamp album, various American atlases, and the gazetteers in the dictionaries had agreed on eight square miles. Hachette and Larousse turned out to agree rather on 150 hectares, or less than three fifths of a square mile. A subsequent check of the Britannica (eleventh edition) revealed arresting detail: "Area about 8 sq. m., the length being 2¼ m. and the width varying from 165 to 1100 yds." Even this arithmetical absurdity had not prevented the producers of all those other reference books from copying the figure of eight square miles, if the Britannica was their source. We are happy to report that the myth broke at last and the "sources" subsequently consulted converged on 0.59 square miles. There is even a new alertness: 0.71 is now reported, because of 76 acres lately reclaimed from the sea. But there is very likely some unwarranted figure on another topic that we are all accepting still, or even newly.

The policy of seeking safety in numbers by checking multiple sources is an excellent precaution; but, as the above example illustrates, it can fail when the sources are not independent. No one would check a newspaper report by checking more copies of the same newspaper. There is a saying that 4×10^7 Frenchmen can't be wrong, but the contrary is the case if they all believe what one wrong Frenchman tells them. In the foregoing example, admittedly, the Frenchmen were right.

For many claims, the typical endorsement is that they are "common knowledge." This is apt to be said of whatever is regarded by large numbers of persons to be true and by almost no one to be false. Preponderance of believers over disbelievers, rather than over nonbelievers, is what is in point, because it is nonbelief, not disbelief, that ignorance breeds. And on almost any subject there are many who have managed to remain ignorant. Now this question: Do we give sufficient backing to a claim by finding that it is widely accepted as true and scarcely ever rejected as false?

What backing suffices depends on what it is to suffice for. In everyday exchanges we are inclined to accept without further issue what we take to be common knowledge. Indeed, we declare our acceptance in so describing it, since to speak of something as known is to speak of it as true. But if the issue is one that we care about, it might be instructive to determine the composition of the segment of the population that holds the belief. It might also be helpful to know how they came to hold it, and whether it concerns matters on which we should expect them to be well-informed. But more important still is the question of the belief's source, and of how, if at all, it was first established. What kinds of evidence would have been appropriate for it and were such grounds available, in the first instance, for its support? For planethood of Neptune there was the investigation of astronomers; for depth of the Pacific the researches of oceanographers; for Hannibal's Alpine excursion the writings of his day and their verification by historians; for the Pythagorean theorem the deductions of mathematicians; for the superiority of one species of can opener over another the long and suffering experience of housewives. Some items of common knowledge, like the last two, we can verify afresh, needing only a little mathematics on the one hand and a few utensils on the other. Others not, though we can still consult authority. What stands open to fresh verification may merit special confidence, since such a belief has been withstanding greater risk of disproof. Thus, in the case of what we ourselves are in poor position to verify, continuing acceptance of it by those in better position might be our touchstone.

But as a touchstone it is fallible. The long and remarkable history of theories having the sun revolve about the
earth may serve as a chastening reminder. If anything
was ever taken to be common knowledge, the geocentric
view certainly qualified in its time. And it had a long
time, centuries over which it was repaired and repaired
again but never discarded. Here the attitude of conservatism toward belief, on balance a helpful attitude, served to
hinder. Nor can we dismiss this misbelief as one that was
based on insufficient investigation; at the time it seemed
well supported from both the experiential and philosophic
poles. That a substance called the ether filled all space was
basic to the physics of a hundred years ago; yet this too
came to be abandoned. And who doubts that it was once
very generally supposed that air transportation for beings
so badly equipped for it as humans was only to be had in
flights of fancy?

The reason such widespread misbeliefs can thrive is
that the ignorance of relevant truths is often accompanied
by ignorance of that ignorance. So we must recognize that
there are almost certain to be many items of today's so-
called common knowledge, some springing directly from
science and some not, that will illustrate the follies of our
age in the next century's textbooks. We like to believe that
much of what we hold in common is firmly established
and will stand as long as there are people to believe it.
Probably we are justified in such confidence. But almost
certainly too, if the intellectual history of our species be
any guide at all, much of what we hold in common will
come to be repudiated. The lesson is one not of despair, but
of humility.

One is sometimes called upon, notably in religion, to
believe testimony in the face of strong contrary evidence.
The Danish philosopher Kierkegaard remarked that the

ability to do this is a test of one's faith. His ancient predecessor Tertullian even abjured reason altogether, declar-
ing "I believe because it is absurd." Believing an absurdity
is already cause for alarm, but believing it because it is
absurd is incoherent. One interpretation is that he meant
merely that some of his beliefs depended on faith because,
being absurd, they were not supported by common sense.
Even thus charitably interpreted, however, Tertullian's
declaration is still a confession of faith in the absurd.

The thought surfaces again in Lewis Carroll.

> "I can't believe that!" said Alice.
> "Can't you?" the Queen said in a pitying tone. "Try again:
> draw a long breath, and shut your eyes."
> Alice laughed. "There's no use trying," she said: "one
> *can't* believe impossible things."
> "I dare say you haven't had much practice," said the
> Queen. "When I was your age I always did it for half-an-
> hour a day. Why, sometimes I've believed as many as six
> impossible things before breakfast."

Alice's was a good philosophical challenge, to Tertullian
and Kierkegaard no less than to the White Queen. "One
can't believe impossible things." Better: one can't believe
a thing if one sees that it is impossible. The point was
stressed early in these pages; we saw it as the very reason
for taking thought, for sifting evidence and revising one's
system of beliefs. When conflicts arise, creating impossible combinations, we cannot rest with them; we have to
resolve them.

One can utter a patent absurdity, certainly, a self-contra-
diction. One can add the words "I believe it," all in
a solemn mood and with no intent to deceive. But
surely there is more to belief than lip service, however
solemn.

The passage from Lewis Carroll brings out also the idea of *trying* to believe something. This is an odd idea even apart from believing the impossible. It is not new. It underlies what is commonly known, in a perhaps unfair attribution to the seventeenth-century mathematician, as Pascal's wager. If God does not exist, we can still believe in Him with impunity; but if He does exist, we doubt Him at our peril; therefore it is the counsel of prudence to believe in God.

There are reasons for *wanting* to believe something. The foregoing is a valid example of that. But how do you *try?* Not by taking a deep breath and closing the eyes. A more effective way is by casting about for favorable evidence. If it outweighs such unfavorable evidence as may turn up, or if wishful thinking saves you from noticing the unfavorable evidence, then your will to believe is crowned with success. But the overlooking of the unfavorable evidence must not be conscious; that way lies mere lip service again, not real belief. And clearly the effort is doomed to failure if you see that the belief is absurd.

Yet it must be said that we do quite reasonably believe some claims in the face of strong contrary evidence, and this is indeed, as Kierkegaard said, a test of our faith. It is a test of our faith in the claimant, and the belief is reasonable if that contrary evidence is outweighed by still stronger evidence underlying that faith. Science is rich in examples.

Einstein claimed that the distance between two flashes depends on the velocity of the vantage point from which the flashes are reported. He claimed that the lapse of time between the flashes is similarly dependent. There will be more time and less distance between the flashes according to one vantage point than according to another. This trade-off between space and time offends common sense, but we accept it on faith in the experts.

Einstein claimed further that the speed of a ray of light is the same from any vantage point; the moving vantage point cannot, in pursuing the light ray, diminish the relative velocity. This again we accept on faith, for all its antecedent absurdity. Another case in point is our open-mindedness toward the extravagant theory of the big bang and the expanding universe: the theory that the universe exploded from a point and has been expanding ever since, with its periphery hurtling outward at the speed of light.

Absurdity is a matter of degree; some statements are more absurd than others. More important, the absurdity of a statement can vary in degree under the pressures and tensions of related beliefs. One cannot properly be said to believe anything that one considers absurd, but one can believe something that one previously considered absurd. The cases noted above from physical science all illustrate this. What had seemed absurd became credible, and hence no longer absurd, by force of expert testimony.

This is the way, also, to look upon Kierkegaard and Tertullian, if not the White Queen: they are believing what had seemed absurd but became credible on the strength of high authority. This is the way to look upon them, that is, if they were really believing and not just deceiving themselves with pious lip service. But we may wonder, still, what evidence they could hope to muster in support of their faith in their sources.

The faith that we place in the scientific experts, at any rate, is well grounded in evidence. Any educated layman has some acquaintance with the kind of thought that goes into scientific experiments and hypotheses and into the mathematics that binds the theory together. Even the uneducated layman must be impressed by the technological fruits of scientific knowledge, from the horseless carriage to the hydrogen bomb and the transmission of pictures from Mars. The expert's grasp is visibly firm, for good or ill. The strength of our belief in the claims of scientists may reasonably grade off with the degree of agreement among the scientists themselves, insofar as we can guess it; thus we may remain more tentative on the big bang than on Einstein's relativity. We may retain yet graver doubts regarding unidentified flying objects, and frank disbelief regarding horoscopes; for here we have no evidence of the trustworthiness of the sources of testimony. And in the case of horoscopes we have strong evidence contrary to the claims themselves: a poor track record in prediction (to the extent that intelligible prediction is at all discernible in horoscopes), dubious value in explanation, and, in the light of our other knowledge, utter implausibility of underlying theory. Acceptability depends, as always, on a weighing of the total evidence.

Chapter VI

Hypothesis

Some philosophers once held that whatever was true could in principle be proved from self-evident beginnings by self-evident steps. The trait of absolute demonstrability, which we attributed to the truths of logic in a narrow sense and to relatively little else, was believed by those philosophers to pervade all truth. They thought that but for our intellectual limitations we could find proofs for any truths, and so, in particular, predict the future to any desired extent. These philosophers were the rationalists. Other philosophers, a little less sanguine, had it that whatever was true could be proved by self-evident steps from two-fold beginnings: self-evident truths and observations. Philosophers of both schools, the rationalists and the somewhat less sanguine ones as well, strained toward their ideals by construing self-evidence every bit as broadly as they in conscience might, or somewhat more so.

Actually even the truths of elementary number theory are presumably not in general derivable, we noted, by self-evident steps from self-evident truths. We owe this insight to Godel's theorem, which was not known to the old-time philosophers.

What then of the truths of nature? Might these be derivable still by self-evident steps from self-evident truths together with observations? Surely not. Take the humblest generalization from observation: that giraffes are mute, that sea water tastes of salt. We infer these from our observations of giraffes and sea water because we expect instinctively that what is true of all observed samples is true of the rest. The principle involved here, far from being self-evident, does not always lead to true generalizations. It worked for the giraffes and the sea water, but it would have let us down if we had inferred from a hundred observations of swans that all swans are white.

Such generalizations already exceed what can be proved from observations and self-evident truths by self-evident steps. Yet such generalizations are still only a small part of natural science. Theories of molecules and atoms are not related to any observations in the direct way in which the generalizations about giraffes and sea water are related to observations of mute giraffes and salty sea water.

It is now recognized that deduction from self-evident truths and observation is not the sole avenue to truth nor even to reasonable belief. A dominant further factor, in solid science as in daily life, is *hypothesis*. In a word, hypothesis is guesswork; but it can be enlightened guesswork.

It is the part of scientific rigor to recognize hypothesis as hypothesis and then to make the most of it. Having accepted the fact that our observations and our self-evi-

dent truths do not together suffice to predict the future, we
frame hypotheses to make up the shortage.

Calling a belief a hypothesis says nothing as to what the
belief is about, how firmly it is held, or how well founded
it is. Calling it a hypothesis suggests rather what sort of
reason we have for adopting or entertaining it. People
adopt or entertain a hypothesis because it would explain,
if it were true, some things that they already believe. Its
evidence is seen in its consequences. For example, consider again the detective thriller in Chapter II. We were
concerned in those pages with change of belief on the
strength of new evidence. But how should we have regarded, in the first place, the belief which the new evidence led us to abandon? It was a hypothesis. It was the
belief that Cabot committed the murder, and it was, for a
while, the best hypothesis we could devise to explain such
circumstances as the killing, the undisturbed state of the
victim's effects, the record of Abbott in the hotel register,
and the testimony of Babbitt's brother-in-law. And then,
when Cabot was discovered on television, what we did
was to try to devise a plausible new hypothesis that would
explain the enlarged array of circumstances.

Hypothesis, where successful, is a two-way street, ex-
tending back to explain the past and forward to predict the
future. What we try to do in framing hypotheses is to
explain some otherwise unexplained happenings by inventing a plausible story, a plausible description or history of relevant portions of the world. What counts in
favor of a hypothesis is a question not to be lightly answered. We may note five virtues that a hypothesis may
enjoy in varying degrees.

Virtue I is *conservatism.* In order to explain the happenings that we are inventing it to explain, the hypothesis
may have to conflict with some of our previous beliefs; but
the fewer the better. Acceptance of a hypothesis is of

course like acceptance of any belief in that it demands rejection of whatever conflicts with it. The less rejection of prior beliefs required, the more plausible the hypothesis—other things being equal.

Often some hypothesis is available that conflicts with no prior beliefs. Thus we may attribute a click at the door to arrival of mail through the slot. Conservatism usually prevails in such a case; one is not apt to be tempted by a hypothesis that upsets prior beliefs when there is no need to resort to one. When the virtue of conservatism deserves notice, rather, is when something happens that cannot evidently be reconciled with our prior beliefs.

There could be such a case when our friend the amateur magician tells us what card we have drawn. How did he do it? Perhaps by luck, one chance in fifty-two; but this conflicts with our reasonable belief, if all unstated, that he would not have volunteered a performance that depended on that kind of luck. Perhaps the cards were marked; but this conflicts with our belief that he had had no access to them, they being ours. Perhaps he peeked or pushed, with help of a sleight-of-hand; but this conflicts with our belief in our perceptiveness. Perhaps he resorted to telepathy or clairvoyance; but this would wreak havoc with our whole web of belief. The counsel of conservatism is the sleight-of-hand.

Conservatism is rather effortless on the whole, having inertia in its favor. But it is sound strategy too, since at each step it sacrifices as little as possible of the evidential support, whatever that may have been, that our overall system of beliefs has hitherto been enjoying. The truth may indeed be radically remote from our present system of beliefs, so that we may need a long series of conservative steps to attain what might have been attained in one rash leap. The longer the leap, however, the more serious an angular error in the direction. For a leap in the dark the likelihood of a happy landing is severely limited. Conservatism holds out the advantages of limited liability and a maximum of live options for each next move.

Virtue II, closely akin to conservatism, is _modesty._ One hypothesis is more modest than another if it is weaker in a logical sense: if it is implied by the other, without implying it. A hypothesis *A* is more modest than *A* and *B* as a joint hypothesis. Also, one hypothesis is more modest than another if it is more humdrum: that is, if the events that it assumes to have happened are of a more usual and familiar sort, hence more to be expected.

Thus suppose a man rings our telephone and ends by apologizing for dialing the wrong number. We will guess that he slipped, rather than that he was a burglar checking to see if anyone was home. It is the more modest of the two hypotheses, butterfingers being rife. We could be wrong, for crime is rife too. But still the butterfingers hypothesis scores better on modesty than the burglar hypothesis, butterfingers being rifer.

We habitually practice modesty, all unawares, when we identify recurrent objects. Unhesitatingly we recognize our car off there where we parked it, though it may have been towed away and another car of the same model may have happened to pull in at that spot. Ours is the more modest hypothesis, because staying put is a more usual and familiar phenomenon than the alternative combination.

It tends to be the counsel of modesty that the lazy world is the likely world. We are to assume as little activity as will suffice to account for appearances. This is not all there is to modesty. It does not apply to the preferred hypothesis in the telephone example, since Mr. Butterfingers is not assumed to be a less active man than one who might have plotted burglary. Modesty figured there merely in keeping the assumptions down, rather than in actually assuming inactivity. In the example of the parked car, however, the modest hypothesis does expressly assume there to be less activity than otherwise. This is a policy that guides science as well as common sense. It is even erected into an explicit principle of mechanics under the name of the law of least action.

Between modesty and conservatism there is no call to draw a sharp line. But by Virtue I we meant conservatism only in a literal sense—conservation of past beliefs. Thus there remain grades of modesty still to choose among even when Virtue I—compatibility with previous beliefs—is achieved to perfection; for both a slight hypothesis and an extravagant one might be compatible with all previous beliefs.

Modesty grades off in turn into Virtue III, *simplicity*. Where simplicity considerations become especially vivid is in drawing curves through plotted points on a graph. Consider the familiar practice of plotting measurements. Distance up the page represents altitude above sea level, for instance, and distance across represents the temperature of boiling water. We plot our measurements on the graph, one dot for each pair. However many points we plot, there remain infinitely many curves that may be drawn through them. Whatever curve we draw represents our generalization from the data, our prediction of what boiling temperatures would be found at altitudes as yet untested. And the curve we will choose to draw is the simplest curve that passes through or reasonably close to all the plotted points.

There is a premium on simplicity in any hypothesis, but the highest premium is on simplicity in the giant joint hypothesis that is science, or the particular science, as a whole. We cheerfully sacrifice simplicity of a part for greater simplicity of the whole when we see a way of doing so. Thus consider gravity. Heavy objects tend

downward: here is an exceedingly simple hypothesis, or
even a mere definition. However, we complicate matters
by accepting rather the hypothesis that the heavy objects
around us are slightly attracted also by one another, and
by the neighboring mountains, and by the moon, and that
all these competing forces detract slightly from the downward one. Newton propounded this more complicated hypothesis even though, aside from tidal effects of the moon,
he had no means of detecting the competing forces; for it
meant a great gain in the simplicity of physics as a whole.
His hypothesis of universal gravitation, which has each
body attracting each in proportion to mass and inversely
as the square of the distance, was what enabled him to
make a single neat system of celestial and terrestrial mechanics.

A modest hypothesis that was long supported both by
theoretical considerations and by observation is that the
trajectory of a projectile is a parabola. A contrary hypothesis is that the trajectory deviates imperceptibly from a
parabola, constituting rather one end of an ellipse whose
other end extends beyond the center of the earth. This
hypothesis is less modest, but again it conduces to a
higher simplicity: Newton's laws of motion and, again,
of gravitation. The trajectories are brought into har-
mony with Kepler's law of the elliptical orbits of the
planets.

Another famous triumph of this kind was achieved by
Count Rumford and later physicists when they showed
how the relation of gas pressure to temperature could be
accounted for by the impact of oscillating particles, for in
this way they reduced the theory of gases to the general
laws of motion. Such was the kinetic theory of gases. In
order to achieve it they had to add the hypothesis, by no
means a modest one, that gas consists of oscillating particles or molecules; but the addition is made up for, and

much more, by the gain in simplicity accruing to physics as a whole.

What is simplicity? For curves we can make good sense of it in geometrical terms. A simple curve is continuous, and among continuous curves the simplest are perhaps those whose curvature changes most gradually from point to point. When scientific laws are expressed in equations, as they so often are, we can make good sense of simplicity in terms of what mathematicians call the degree of an equation, or the order of a differential equation. This line was taken by Sir Harold Jeffreys. The lower the degree, the lower the order, and the fewer the terms, the simpler the equation. Such simplicity ratings of equations agree with the simplicity ratings of curves when the equations are plotted as in analytical geometry.

Simplicity is harder to define when we turn away from curves and equations. Sometimes in such cases it is not to be distinguished from modesty. Commonly a hypothesis *A* will count as simpler than *A* and *B* together; thus far simplicity and modesty coincide. On the other hand the simplicity gained by Newton's hypothesis of universal gravitation was not modesty, in the sense that we have assigned to that term; for the hypothesis was not logically implied by its predecessors, nor was it more humdrum in respect of the events that it assumed. Newton's hypothesis was simpler than its predecessors in that it covered in a brief unified story what had previously been covered only by two unrelated accounts. Similar remarks apply to the kinetic theory of gases.

In the notion of simplicity there is a nagging subjectivity. What makes for a brief unified story depends on the structure of our language, after all, and on our available vocabulary, which need not reflect the structure of nature. This subjectivity of simplicity is puzzling, if simplicity in hypotheses is to make for plausibility. Why should the subjectively simpler of two hypotheses stand a better chance of predicting objective events? Why should we expect nature to submit to our subjective standards of simplicity?

That would be too much to expect. Physicists and others are continually finding that they have to complicate their theories to accommodate new data. At each stage, however, when choosing a hypothesis subject to subsequent correction, it is still best to choose the simplest that is not yet excluded. This strategy recommends itself on much the same grounds as the strategies of conservatism and modesty. The longer the leap, we reflected, the more and wilder ways of going wrong. But likewise, the more complex the hypothesis, the more and wilder ways of going wrong; for how can we tell which complexities to adopt? Simplicity, like conservatism and modesty, limits liability. Conservatism can be good strategy even though one's present theory be ever so far from the truth, and simplicity can be good strategy even though the world be ever so complicated. Our steps toward the complicated truth can usually be laid out most dependably if the simplest hypothesis that is still tenable is chosen at each step. It has even been argued that this policy will lead us at least asymptotically toward a theory that is true.

There is more, however, to be said for simplicity: the simplest hypothesis often just is the likeliest, apparently, quite apart from questions of cagy strategy. Why should this be? There is a partial explanation in our ways of keeping score on predictions. The predictions based on the simpler hypotheses tend to be scored more leniently. Thus consider curves, where simplicity comparisons are so clear. If a curve is kinky and complex, and if some measurement predicted from the curve turns out to miss the mark by a distance as sizable as some of the kinks of the curve itself, we will count the prediction a failure. We will feel that so kinky a curve, if correct, would have had a kink to catch this wayward point. On the other hand, a miss of the same magnitude might be excused if the curve were smooth and simple. It might be excused as due to inaccuracy of measurement or to some unexplained local interference. This cynical doctrine of selective leniency is very plausible in the case of the curves. And we may reasonably expect a somewhat similar but less easily pictured selectivity to be at work in the interest of the simple hypotheses where curves are not concerned.

Considering how subjective our standards of simplicity are, we wondered why we should expect nature to submit to them. Our first answer was that we need not expect it; the strategy of favoring the simple at each step is good anyway. Now we have noted further that some of nature's seeming simplicity is an effect of our bookkeeping. Are we to conclude that the favoring of simplicity is entirely our doing, and that nature is neutral in the matter? Not quite. Darwin's theory of natural selection offers a causal connection between subjective simplicity and objective truth in the following way. Innate subjective standards of simplicity that make people prefer some hypotheses to others will have survival value insofar as they favor successful prediction. Those who predict best are likeliest to survive and reproduce their kind, in a state of nature anyway, and so their innate standards of simplicity are handed down. Such standards will also change in the light of experience, becoming still better adapted to the growing body of science in the course of the individual's lifetime. (But these improvements do not get handed down genetically.)

Virtue IV is *generality*. The wider the range of application of a hypothesis, the more general it is. When we find electricity conducted by a piece of copper wire, we leap to the hypothesis that all copper, not just long thin copper, conducts electricity.

The plausibility of a hypothesis depends largely on how compatible the hypothesis is with our being observers placed at random in the world. Funny coincidences often occur, but they are not the stuff that plausible hypotheses are made of. The more general the hypothesis is by which we account for our present observation, the less of a coincidence it is that our present observation should fall under it. Hence, in part, the power of Virtue IV to confer plausibility.

The possibility of testing a hypothesis by repeatable experiment presupposes that the hypothesis has at least some share of Virtue IV. For in a repetition of an experiment the test situation can never be exactly what it was for the earlier run of the experiment; and so, if both runs are to be relevant to the hypothesis, the hypothesis must be at least general enough to apply to both test situations.[1] One would of course like to have it much more general still.

Virtues I, II, and III made for plausibility. So does Virtue IV to some degree, we see, but that is not its main claim; indeed generality conflicts with modesty. But generality is desirable in that it makes a hypothesis interesting and important if true.

We lately noted a celebrated example of generality in Newton's hypothesis of universal gravitation, and another in the kinetic theory of gases. It is no accident that the same illustrations should serve for both simplicity and generality. Generality without simplicity is cold comfort. Thus take celestial mechanics with its elliptical orbits, and take also terrestrial mechanics with its parabolic trajectories, just take them in tandem as a bipartite theory of motion. If the two together cover everything covered by Newton's unified laws of motion, then generality is no

---

[1] We are indebted to Nell E. Scroggins for suggesting this point.

ground for preferring Newton's theory to the two taken together. But Virtue III, simplicity, is. When a way is seen of gaining great generality with little loss of simplicity, or great simplicity with no loss of generality, then conservatism and modesty give way to scientific revolution.

The aftermath of the famous Michelson-Morley experiment of 1887 is a case in point. The purpose of this delicate and ingenious experiment was to measure the speed with which the earth travels through the ether. For two centuries, from Newton onward, it had been a well entrenched tenet that something called the ether pervaded all of what we think of as empty space. The great physicist Lorentz (1853–1928) had hypothesized that the ether itself was stationary. What the experiment revealed was that the method that was expected to enable measurement of the earth's speed through the ether was totally inadequate to that task. Supplementary hypotheses multiplied in an attempt to explain the failure without seriously disrupting the accepted physics. Lorentz, in an effort to save the hypothesis of stationary ether, shifted to a new and more complicated set of formulas in his mathematical physics. Einstein soon cut through all this, propounding what is called the special theory of relativity.

This was a simplification of physical theory. Not that Einstein's theory is as simple as Newton's had been; but Newton's physics had been shown untenable by the Michelson-Morley experiment. The point is that Einstein's theory is simpler than Newton's as corrected and supplemented and complicated by Lorentz and others. It was a glorious case of gaining simplicity at the sacrifice of conservatism; for the time-honored ether went by the board, and far older and more fundamental tenets went by the board too. Drastic changes were made in our conception of the very structure of space and time, as noted in Chapter V.

Yet let the glory not blind us to Virtue I. (When our estrangement from the past is excessive, the imagination boggles; genius is needed to devise the new theory, and high talent is needed to find one's way about in it. Even Einstein's revolution, moreover, had its conservative strain; Virtue I was not wholly sacrificed. The old physics of Newton's classical mechanics is, in a way, preserved after all.) For the situations in which the old and the new theories would predict contrary observations are situations that we are not apt to encounter without sophisticated experiment—because of their dependence on exorbitant velocities or exorbitant distances. This is why classical mechanics held the field so long. Whenever, even having switched to Einstein's relativity theory, we dismiss those exorbitant velocities and distances for the purpose of some practical problem, promptly the discrepancy between Einstein's theory and Newton's becomes too small to matter. Looked at from this angle, Einstein's theory takes on the aspect not of a simplification but a generalization. We might say that the sphere of applicability of Newtonian mechanics in its original simplicity was shown, by the Michelson-Morley experiment and related results, to be less than universal; and then Einstein's theory comes as a generalization, presumed to hold universally. Within its newly limited sphere, Newtonian mechanics retains its old utility. What is more, the evidence of past centuries for Newtonian mechanics even carries over, within these limits, as evidence for Einstein's physics; for, as far as it goes, it fits both.

What is thus illustrated by Einstein's relativity is more modestly exemplified elsewhere, and generally aspired to: the retention, in some sense, of old theories in new ones. If the new theory can be so fashioned as to diverge from the old only in ways that are undetectable in most ordinary circumstances, then it inherits the evidence of the old theory rather than having to overcome it. Such is the force of conservatism even in the context of revolution.

Virtues I through IV may be further illustrated by considering Neptune. That Neptune is among the planets is readily checked by anyone with reference material; indeed it passes as common knowledge, and there is for most of us no need to check it. But only through extensive application of optics and geometry was it possible to determine, in the first instance, that the body we call Neptune exists, and that it revolves around the sun. This required not only much accumulated science and mathematics, but also powerful telescopes and cooperation among scientists.

In fact it happens that Neptune's existence and planethood were strongly suspected even before that planet was observed. Physical theory made possible the calculation of what the orbit of the planet Uranus should be, but Uranus' path differed measurably from its calculated course. Now the theory on which the calculations were based was, like all theories, open to revision or refutation. But here conservatism operates: one is loath to revise extensively a well established set of beliefs, especially a set so deeply entrenched as a basic portion of physics. And one is even more loath to abandon as spurious immense numbers of observation reports made by serious scientists. Given that Uranus had been observed to be as much as two minutes of arc from its calculated position, what was sought was a discovery that would render this deviation explicable within the framework of accepted theory. Then the theory and its generality would be unimpaired, and the new complexity would be minimal.

It would have been possible in principle to speculate that some special characteristic of Uranus exempted that planet from the physical laws that are followed by other planets. If such a hypothesis had been resorted to, Neptune would not have been discovered; not then, at any rate. There was a reason, however, for not resorting to such a hypothesis. It would have been what is called an *ad hoc hypothesis,* and ad hoc hypotheses are bad air, for they are wanting in Virtues III and IV. Ad hoc hypotheses are hypotheses that purport to account for some particular observations by supposing some very special forces to be at work in the particular cases at hand, and not generalizing sufficiently beyond those cases. The vice of an ad hoc hypothesis admits of degrees. The extreme case is where the hypothesis covers only the observations it was invented to account for, so that it is totally useless in prediction. Then also it is insusceptible of confirmation, which would come of our verifying its predictions.

Another example that has something of the implausibility of an ad hoc hypothesis is the water-diviner's belief that a willow wand held above the ground can be attracted by underground water. The force alleged is too special. One feels, most decidedly, the lack of an intelligible mechanism to explain the attraction. And what counts as intelligible mechanism? A hypothesis strikes us as giving an intelligible mechanism when the hypothesis rates well in familiarity, generality, simplicity. We attain the ultimate in intelligibility of mechanism, no doubt, when we see how to explain something in terms of physical impact, or the familiar and general laws of motion.

There is an especially notorious sort of hypothesis which, whether or not properly classified also as ad hoc, shares the traits of insusceptibility of confirmation and uselessness in prediction. This is the sort of hypothesis that seeks to save some other hypothesis from refutation by systematically excusing the failures of its predictions. When the Voice from Beyond is silent despite the incantations of the medium, we may be urged to suppose that "someone in the room is interfering with the communication." In an effort to save the prior hypothesis that certain incantations will summon forth the Voice, the auxiliary hypothesis that untoward thoughts can thwart audible signals is advanced. This auxiliary hypothesis is no wilder than the hypothesis that it was invoked to save, and thus an uncritical person may find the newly wrinkled theory no harder to accept than its predecessor had been. On the other hand the critical observer sees that evidence has ceased altogether to figure. Experimental failure is being milked to fatten up theory.

These reflections bring a fifth virtue to the fore: _refutability_, Virtue V. It seems faint praise of a hypothesis to call it refutable. But the point, we have now seen, is approximately this: some imaginable event, recognizable if it occurs, must suffice to refute the hypothesis. Otherwise the hypothesis predicts nothing, is confirmed by nothing, and confers upon us no earthly good beyond perhaps a mistaken peace of mind.

This is too simple a statement of the matter. Just about any hypothesis, after all, can be held unrefuted no matter what, by making enough adjustments in other beliefs—though sometimes doing so requires madness. We think loosely of a hypothesis as implying predictions when, strictly speaking, the implying is done by the hypothesis together with a supporting chorus of ill-distinguished background beliefs. It is done by the whole relevant theory taken together.

Properly viewed, therefore, Virtue V is a matter of degree, as are its four predecessors. The degree to which a hypothesis partakes of Virtue V is measured by the cost of retaining the hypothesis in the face of imaginable events. The degree is measured by how dearly we cherish the previous beliefs that would have to be sacrificed to save the hypothesis. The greater the sacrifice, the more refutable the hypothesis.

A prime example of deficiency in respect of Virtue V is astrology. Astrologers can so hedge their predictions that they are devoid of genuine content. We may be told that a person will "tend to be creative" or "tend to be outgoing," where the evasiveness of a verb and the fuzziness of adjectives serve to insulate the claim from repudiation. But even if a prediction should be regarded as a failure, astrological devotees can go on believing that the stars rule our destinies; for there is always some item of information, perhaps as to a planet's location at a long gone time, that may be alleged to have been overlooked. Conflict with other beliefs thus need not arise.

All our contemplating of special virtues of hypotheses will not, we trust, becloud the fact that the heart of the matter is observation. Virtues I through V are guides to the framing of hypotheses that, besides conforming to past observations, may plausibly be expected to conform to future ones. When they fail on the latter score, questions are reopened. Thus it was that the Michelson-Morley experiment led to modifications, however inelegant, of Newton's physics at the hands of Lorentz. When Einstein came out with a simpler way of accommodating past observations, moreover, his theory was no mere reformulation of the Newton-Lorentz system; it was yet a third theory, different in some of its predicted observations and answerable to them. Its superior simplicity brought plausibility to its distinctive consequences.

Hypotheses were to serve two purposes: to explain the past and predict the future. Roughly and elliptically speaking, the hypothesis serves these purposes by implying the past events that it was supposed to explain, and by implying future ones. More accurately speaking, as we saw, what does the implying is the whole relevant theory taken together, as newly revised by adoption of the hypothesis in question. Moreover, the predictions that are implied are mostly not just simple predictions of future observations or other events; more often they are conditional predictions. The hypothesis will imply that we will make these further observations if we look in such and such a place, or take other feasible steps. If the predictions come out right, we can win bets or gain other practical advantages. Also, when they come out right, we gain confirmatory evidence for our hypotheses. When they come out wrong, we go back and tinker with our hypotheses and try to make them better.

What we called limiting principles in Chapter IV are, when intelligible, best seen as hypotheses—some good, some bad. Similarly, of course, for scientific laws generally. And similarly for laws of geometry, set theory, and other parts of mathematics. All these laws—those of physics and those of mathematics equally—are among the component hypotheses that fit together to constitute our inclusive scientific theory of the world. The most general hypotheses tend to be the least answerable to any particular observation, since subsidiary hypotheses can commonly be juggled and adjusted to accommodate conflicts; and on this score of aloofness there is no clear boundary between theoretical physics and mathematics. Of course hypotheses in various fields of inquiry may tend to receive their confirmation from different kinds of investigation, but this should in no way conflict with our seeing them all as hypotheses.

We talk of framing hypotheses. Actually we inherit the main ones, growing up as we do in a going culture. The continuity of belief is due to the retention, at each particular time, of most beliefs. In this retentiveness science even at its most progressive is notably conservative. Virtue I looms large. A reasonable person will look upon some of his or her retained beliefs as self-evident, on others as common knowledge though not self-evident, on others as vouched for by authority in varying degree, and on others as hypotheses that have worked all right so far.

But the going culture goes on, and each of us participates in adding and dropping hypotheses. Continuity makes the changes manageable. Disruptions that are at all sizable are the work of scientists, but we all modify the fabric in our small way, as when we conclude on indirect evidence that the schools will be closed and the planes grounded or that an umbrella thought to have been forgotten by one person was really forgotten by another.

Chapter VII

Induction, Analogy, and Intuition

Why do we expect toothpaste to exude when we squeeze the tube? We could cite general principles about what happens to liquids or soft solids under pressure, but we are more likely to support our expectation in terms of our past experience with tubes and their squeezings. What happens in such simple activities is related to general principles only in ways which, for most of us, remain far in the background. Very far; for were toothpaste to fail to spurt forth on a given squeezing we would surely not want to rewrite our physics. We would consider such hypotheses as that the toothpaste in the tube had been used up, that it was blocked in its passage by some foreign object, or that it had hardened. We would explain a failure of our expectation in the least sweeping terms available, making the revision in our belief body as small as possible. We would maximize Virtues I and II of Chapter VI: conservatism and modesty.

We expect the toothpaste mainly because prior squeezings have produced toothpaste. Such is very commonly the way of our expectations. We support our expectations —our beliefs about the future—by appeal to what is past. If Western sagas have always been seen to resolve their seemingly insuperable problems just moments before the end of scheduled air time, we expect the next Western saga we view to do so. If Bullwhip Fudgies have again and again, without fail, inserted their advertisement in the middle of the weekly Lionel Flemm Hour, we expect them to do so when next we tune in that program. Such expectation could indeed be forestalled, as by a newspaper headline "Bullwhip Unloads Flemm." Or we might simply be disappointed in our expectation on some occasion. Normally we are less than certain how things will go in the future, no matter how extensive our backlog of experience. Among the expectations that have their share of support are those that bid us brace for surprises.

More may contribute to our expectations than mere counting of cases. We perhaps come to see the rationale of the program's achieving resolution while air time, but not too much of it, lasts. Given what we suppose to be the purpose of its producers, what we have observed falls into a scheme of things. So it is with our beliefs pretty generally: they partially support one another by partially explaining one another. But, even so, what we come to believe derives much of its support from the sheer bulk of past cases. This simple and unimaginative source of belief is a factor that is central to the process of learning from experience and it needs to be isolated for consideration.

This central factor is the expectation that future cases will work out like past ones. It is the attribution of similar behavior to similar things. This familiar method of framing a general hypothesis, by generalizing from observed cases to all cases of the kind, is called *induction*. It is the natural avenue to Virtue IV, generality.

When we try to be a bit more explicit and precise about induction's guiding principle—that future cases will be like past ones—we are suddenly lost in perplexity. The problem has been put in most striking form by the contemporary philosopher Nelson Goodman. Suppose that many emeralds have been examined for color and all have been found green. You may wonder how, failing greenness, we would know that they were emeralds in the first place; but this is not the point of the example. Imagine, so as to get on with Goodman's point, that emeralds have been identified in the dark by a chemical test, and that we are checking on color afterward. Very well, then; since all up to now have proved green, we expect the next emerald examined to be green. However, consider whether the following is a reason to the contrary, and, if not, why not. We adopt a new adjective, "grue", explained as follows: anything is grue if it is examined before midnight tonight, and is green, or else is not examined by then, and is blue. Thus the grue emeralds comprise all those green ones that will have been examined by midnight tonight together with all blue ones, if any, not examined by then. Now since all emeralds so far examined have been examined before midnight tonight, and have been green, it is also true that they have all been grue. We took their greenness to license our expectation that the next to be examined would be green; so then, symmetrically, their grueness should plump for the next one's grueness. Suppose that the next emerald to be examined will not be examined before midnight tonight. It, then, will have to be blue if it is to be grue. Thus we have a paradox: the next emerald is expected to be green since all emeralds examined have been green, but it is also expected to be grue, and therefore blue, since all emeralds examined have been grue.

There is no temptation to expect the next emerald to be blue. It is alarmingly difficult, however, to say why that inference is not legitimate while the inference to greenness is. What more clearly emerges is that to say that we expect future cases to be like past ones is, on its face, to say nothing.

This point is further borne out by a second paradox of induction. If we could fairly infer by induction that future cases will share each trait shared by all past ones, then there would be, for each of us, overwhelming inductive evidence for the solemn proposition that we are living our last moment. For, consider any specific moment. Say, for instance, that 1978 is about to begin. Every moment of one's life thus far has had the trait of being prior to 1978. By induction, then, may one conclude that all moments of one's life will share that trait? This conclusion, if correct, would be one's last.

And yet, if some illogician were to make a habit of these lugubrious inductions, he would find each time that the induction failed; he has always survived. A second-level induction, an induction about such inductions, tells him that such inductions are always wrong. Should he sigh with relief and conclude that he is immortal? He might even have reached this cheerful conclusion more directly, if he had begun in a sanguine frame of mind. For he could simply have observed that every past moment of his life had been followed by further living. By induction he might then have concluded that every moment of his life would be followed by further living, and hence that he would live forever.

The sober fact is that we cannot expect every trait shared by past cases to carry forward to future cases. Some

traits command confident expectation of continuance and
some do not. We expect greenness to carry forward to
further emeralds; grueness not. We do not expect the trait
of being prior to 1978 to carry forward to future moments
without end, and neither do we expect the trait of being
followed by further living to carry forward without end.
Green is *projectible,* as Goodman says, while grue and
these other traits are not. Induction projects the projectible traits into the future, and not the others.

To call a trait projectible is only to say that it is suited
to induction, and not to say why. We may still ask why
some traits should be thus suited, and how to spot them.
We do have a natural knack for spotting such traits, with
better than random success; they are the traits we notice.
Green is a trait that we naturally and unhesitatingly
project from past observation to future expectation; on the
other hand the trait of being prior to 1978 is not such a one,
and neither is the trait of being followed by further living,
and neither is grue. It is significant that we did not have
a word for grue; it is not a trait we notice.

Induction is the expectation that similar things will
behave similarly; better, that things already seen to be
appreciably similar will prove similar in further ways.
The question of what traits are projectible, then, can as
well be put simply thus: What counts as similarity? Everything is similar to everything in some respect. Any
two things share as many traits as any other two, if we are
undiscriminating about what to call a trait; things can be
grouped in no end of arbitrary ways. When we call something more similar to one thing than to another, we are
not counting shared traits indiscriminately; we are counting projectible traits. Sharing greenness counts for similarity; sharing grueness does not. Our eye for
projectibility is our eye for similarity. These are two
names for the same problem. Simplicity, likewise, was

found in Chapter VI to be tinged with subjectivity; surely
it is of a piece with projectibility and similarity. Projectible traits are felt to be simpler than others, as well as
making for similarity.

Induction is not peculiarly intellectual. Essentially it is
just a matter of learning from experience what to expect;
and everyone is at it continually. Other animals are at it
too, in learning what to avoid and where to go for food and
water. All such learning proceeds by similarity, or projection of traits. All of it depends on a prior tendency to
notice certain traits and so to single them out for projection rather than others. Our eye for similarity or projectibility is, at its crudest, part of our animal heritage. And
why should it be so successful? Why should traits like
green, which we have an innate tendency to notice and so
to project, tend also to be the right ones—the ones that
succeed in prediction? To this question, just as to the question of simplicity in Chapter VI, the answer is best sought
in terms of natural selection. An innate sensitivity to certain traits, and insensitivity to others, will have survival
value insofar as the traits that are favored are favorable to
prediction.

Projection of grue has had every bit as much survival
value up to now, Goodman notes, as projection of green. If
a genetic mutation in our ancestry had engendered in us
a neural organization of a kind that encouraged expectation of grue rather than green, our expectations on that
score up to now would have been verified no less well. But
there are limitations, however little understood, to the
varieties of neural organizations that genetic mutations
can render inheritable. A tendency to project green can
evidently be fostered by an inheritable neural organization; a tendency to project grue can probably not. The fact
may be unfortunate, and the stroke of midnight may
prove it so. But the present authors expect not, such being
their inheritance. Science would crumble overnight.

This is not to say that there is an easy answer to Goodman's riddle. Neither the projectible traits nor the traits favored by natural selection are easily characterized, and the relationship between them is more tenuous still. Further, when we appeal to biology and theories of neural organization we appeal to science that is itself grounded, in large measure, inductively. Nor can we ever hope, in examining our basic modes of reasoning, to dissociate ourselves altogether from what is under scrutiny. What does emerge is that our innate sensitivities have served us much better than purely random selection of traits would likely have served us, and that our animal faith bids us expect continuance of our good fortune.

Our native flair for projectible traits does not remain as evolution left it. It develops further in the light of our experience. We can make inductive generalizations concerning the successes and failures of our past inductions, and so decide in effect that certain traits were not so projectible as we had thought. We revise some of our groupings. We read whales out of the tribe of fishes. We fix upon new traits in the light of a developing scientific theory, and find that inductions based on these traits are more successful. Science advances induction as induction advances science.

Induction is not a procedure alternative to hypothesis; it is a case of hypothesis. We called it the natural avenue to Virtue IV, generality. Virtue III, simplicity, is also always present where induction takes place, since projectible traits are felt as simpler than others. Induction is the way not to helter-skelter generality, or Virtue IV alone, but to Virtues IV and III combined.

According to traditional accounts, inference has two main species: deductive and inductive. The inductive, unlike the deductive, proceeds from the less to the more general; it gives you more than you began with. These were looked upon as complementary and symmetrical

ways of justifying knowledge. To pair them thus and picture them as symmetrical, however, is to lose sight of
serious differences. In Chapter IV we reflected briefly on
deductive inference as inference that can be carried out by
a series of self-evident steps. Its central techniques are
studied in logic and are well understood. Methods of inductive inference, on the other hand, are not sharply sepa-
rable from strategies for framing hypotheses generally;
and of such strategies no sharp and satisfactory theory is
to be found, comparable to what logic provides for deduction. What little we shall have to say regarding the evaluation of inductive inference will appear in the next
chapter, where we consider the confirmation and refutation of hypotheses.

Induction, we said, produces a hypothesis by generalization. This description supposes that the inductive conclusion is stated or thought as an explicit general law.
Induction, we also said, is essentially just a matter of
learning what to expect. But this description applies
equally when a prediction or expectation is reached from
past observations directly in a single leap, uninterrupted
by an intervening general statement. Past experience in
boiling lobsters leads us directly to expect the next one to
turn red. Past experience with the dinner bell leads the
dog directly to salivate at the sound of the gong, uninterrupted by an intervening general statement. We might
reserve the term "induction" for inferences where the
conclusion is general and explicit, since we have other
terms for the leap from cases to cases. We have the term
analogy for where the leap is a considered one, and *conditioned reflex* for where it is not.

Thus, the direct relation between our observation of the
redness of past boiled lobsters and our expectation of redness of the next victim is a relation of analogy. The name
of induction can be reserved for our generalization that all

boiled lobsters are red. Again our individual expectations on television, and of the emergence of toothpaste from the squeezed tube, are got by analogy. The corresponding inductions, or general hypotheses, would in ordinary circumstances never be framed at all.

One who derives a belief by analogy need not be prepared to offer any inductive support for it nor even notice that that belief rests on an analogy. It is the way of each of us most of the time to forge new beliefs from old ones without reflecting at all on the arguments that might be summoned in their behalf. Such beliefs may still be eminently reasonable. We form habits of building beliefs much as we form our other habits; only in habits of building beliefs there is less room for idiosyncrasy.

Some analogies that we use are notoriously weak. Perhaps a person hears a new voice and, noticing that the voice resembles that of an old friend, speculates that the voice's owner will be like the old friend in other significant ways. Such an analogy is shadowy, but we all tend at times to build on analogies that are no better. When a feature of a newly encountered person or object strikes a familiar chord it is often fairly instinctive to project to the new person or object what experience has associated with that feature. As a person gains in experience she learns, or should learn, to temper such expectations. She learns to discriminate between associations that are worth building new beliefs on and those that are not. The more people she meets the better she is able to judge what expectations she can base on a person's voice. Her native flair for projectibility is developing in the light of experience and even so she may remain quite unable to articulate any principles for her acquired discrimination. It is much easier to build beliefs and hypotheses than to describe the rationale behind their construction. This is true even where the hypotheses belong to science.

Sometimes, though we are quite convinced that a belief is right, we can think of no reasons at all for holding it. It is in such cases that we are apt to give credit to *intuition*. Some people think of intuition as a mystical source of knowledge—a source disconnected from normal ways of reaching conclusions. They speak of a woman's intuition, as if of a sixth sense. They speak of intuitive people, as if of persons with some special faculty. Happily intuition need not be so regarded. Consider a situation in which we sense that a person is insincere. There may be no known evidence for the belief, but that need not mean that no relevant observations have been made. Perhaps the person hesitated just a fraction of a second before answering some question, or perhaps he momentarily exhibited a certain facial expression. Such things might well have been what led to our suspicion about him, even though they may never have registered as data. This would be analogy at work, though we would not be noticing the process. Our sensing insincerity could rest on our picking up a sensory clue like one once linked with someone believed to be insincere. Not only might we not have noticed the clue; we may even have forgotten the former attribution of insincerity.

The appeal to intuition is explicit and most insistent, understandably, among devotees of doctrines that are short on reasoned support. Really there is no place for an explicit appeal to intuition. Where an intuition has anything at all to be said for it, it has something making no mention of intuition to be said for it: sensory clues that may not have registered as such, long forgotten beliefs, analogies more or less vague. Uncovering the basis of such a belief helps us to appraise the belief; yet to demand that the basis of every reasonable belief be thus uncovered would be to demand the impossible.

Still, when mechanism is unclear there is a lamentable tendency to embellish some scant story in order to take up the slack. This is a tendency that has flourished from earliest times, the tendency to go to any needed lengths of invention rather than face ignorance. It has bestowed literary benefits; it has brought us the gods of many a legend. Nowadays, when offered seriously, the manufactured story is apt to be couched in terms from science to enhance its claim to authority. Modesty, in our sense, may be cast to the winds. Thus we get a full-blown theory of "auras" —tell-tale electromagnetic fields that surround people—to account for cases where we cannot identify our sensory clues in more familiar ways. Even such a theory as that, of course, recognizes that bare appeal to intuition is insufficient as an account of mechanism. For that matter, so does the popular mention of "vibes", though that may be seen as a term with more flavor than content.

Think of our everyday ability to recognize people we know on sight. We may be totally incapable of giving enough description of a person we know well to enable anyone else to recognize him. We just have this uncanny knack. Still no one is inclined to say that we recognize our friends through intuition; it is vaguely set down to experience. We respond to visual clues, organize them in a twinkling, and compare the result with what is stored in memory.

That last phrase is one that is common in talk of computers. And indeed, machines are able to perform certain tasks of recognition. For example, machines can be programmed to discriminate handwritten letters of the alphabet, so that they can read script as well as print. We know how they do it; they compare what is fed into them with what has been internalized in them through programming. The study of such devices belongs to the field called artificial intelligence, which studies how tasks that would normally be thought to require intelligent behavior might be carried out by machines. It seems likely that development of this field will lead to significant gains in psychology. In particular, it should bring heightened understanding of how humans recognize complex objects.

Analogy can lead not only from particular experiences to particular expectations, but also from general hypotheses to general hypotheses. Say we have evidence that a serum prepared from a certain bacterial culture immunizes against the disease caused by those bacteria. If there is a closely related disease caused by bacteria that we regard as very much like those causing the first disease, then we may find it plausible that a correspondingly prepared serum will immunize against the second disease. Our belief about the first serum has its claim to Virtue IV, generality, enhanced if it is extensible to a similar belief about a similar serum. So even in advance of any testing we have reason to look favorably upon the hypothesis about the second serum. What is at work here is still analogy, but it is analogy now between two parallel laws rather than between particulars.

We pictured analogy as by-passing inductive generalizations; as moving directly from similars to similars. Now when the analogy is between general laws there is still the by-passed inductive generalization, but it is at the next higher level of generality. One might afterward try to capture it. In the above example, the generalization would be a comprehensive law to the effect that immunity against each disease of a certain described class is conferred by a serum prepared from the corresponding bacteria. The class would be described by making explicit the similarities that related the two diseases in the original analogy; the class would include all diseases thus related.

Analogy as thus far pictured is an inferential leap, whereof the top of the trajectory is a slurred-over induction. Analogy passes from one instance of a generalization to another without pausing for explicit induction of the generalization. The intervening generalization is slurred over because interest happens to be centered rather upon some particular instance that is to be inferred. Another effect of this allocation of interest is that we are likely to attend to more varied features of the instance that is to be inferred than we would if generality were our objective. Hence the previous instances or premises, from which we are making the analogical inference, are apt to have been so chosen as to share a variety of features with the case to be inferred. On this account, we commonly have to make do with just one previous instance, as in the serum example, unlike the style of proper induction; and the single instance is apt moreover to carry sufficient conviction, thanks to the multiple resemblances. Thus it is that an analogy often looks very unlike a slurred-over induction, and the missing generalization is not always easy to supply.

The word "analogy" is of course often correctly applied to matters other than inference. It is applied to a common way of learning new terms. The concept of a class or set, for instance, is grasped by partial analogy to a heap, and the concept of an atom or electron is grasped by partial analogy to a visible speck. These other uses of the word "analogy" need not concern us. The common core of all the uses is fairly well covered by "similarity" or "parallelism".

Chapter VIII

Confirmation and Refutation

An author of this book experienced headaches accompanied by blurred vision. The first step in trying to find a way of preventing them was to find some explanation. Through a combination of recollection and watchfulness he came to suspect that the headaches were associated with eating sweet pickles, so he framed the hypothesis that the sweet pickles brought on the headaches. Once after thinking of this hypothesis he deliberately indulged himself in sweet pickles, and, to be sure, a headache followed. Abstention from such indulgence was found to coincide with absence of such headaches. He has accepted the hypothesis ever since, avoided sweet pickles, and had no such headaches.

The obvious way of testing a hypothesis is to test its consequences. One sees whether a headache follows the eating of sweet pickles, being prepared to discard, or at least modify, the hypothesis if none does. When a headache does follow, the hypothesis receives confirmation. But its truth is far from established thereby. It has merely withstood one challenge. We noted in Chapter VI that many curves may be drawn through plotted points. This means that no matter how many data we have there will still be many mutually incompatible hypotheses each of which implies those data. What confirms one hypothesis will confirm many; the data are good for a whole sheaf of hypotheses and not just one. This is what makes it necessary for us to have criteria for hypotheses, such as the five Virtues of Chapter VI, above and beyond the requirement that they should imply what we have observed. In terms of the Virtues a hypothesis may excel its rivals sufficiently to be regarded as definitely established.

Confirmation of the pickles hypothesis might have been pursued further. For one thing, the single experiment provided very limited confirmation for the hypothesis; further tests, in varied circumstances, might have been undertaken that would either have brought added confirmation or shown the hypothesis to be mistaken. For another thing, the hypothesis settled on might seem somewhat short on Virtue IV (generality), since it gives no hint as to why one person should so react while other persons appear not to. Thus our sufferer might have sought a refinement of the hypothesis—a refinement that would account for his idiosyncrasy, perhaps by relating particular physiological traits to specific allergic reactions. In view of the sparseness of medical knowledge about such relationships, this would have been hard. Still, a certain plausibility can be claimed for the hypothesis on account of elementary background knowledge—the knowledge that what one eats often brings on unwelcome physical reactions. We build on what we know in order to learn more. Doing this maximizes the chance of finding a workable hypothesis that fits in with the rest of what we accept; thus it serves Virtue I, conservatism. And since using what we already know may lighten the burden on the hypothesis sought and allow it to be a modest one, Virtue II may be served as well.

The pickles hypothesis was imprecise, as are many that suit our everyday purposes. It was imprecise in that it specified no required quantity of sweet pickles and no particular time interval between indulgence and reaction. And the terms in which it was cast were vague, since there can be doubt as to what is to count as a sweet pickle or as a headache of the appropriate kind.

Ordinarily, hypotheses used in science are more precise and less vague than those adopted in everyday affairs. There is for instance the scientific hypothesis or law about the boiling point of water, which says that water free of impurities boils at 100°C. if it is subject to a pressure of 760 millimeters. Measurement itself is of course never wholly precise; but what this hypothesis is meant to give us to expect is that you can bring the boiling point as near as you please to 100°C. by bringing the pressure closer and closer to 760 millimeters and also progressively purifying the water.

Precision might be listed as Virtue VI, supplementary to the five virtues in Chapter VI. Like those virtues, precision conduces to the plausibility of a hypothesis. It does so in an indirect fashion. The more precise a hypothesis is, the more strongly it is confirmed by each successful prediction that it generates. This is because of the relative improbability of coincidences. If a prediction based on a hypothesis just happens to come out true for irrelevant reasons, that is a coincidence; and, the more precise a hypothesis, the less room there is for such a coincidence. If the hypothesis says precisely that the pickles will bring a headache in twelve to thirteen minutes, a confirmatory headache cannot be dismissed lightly as coincidence. If, on the other hand, the hypothesis just says vaguely that the pickles will bring a headache in the fullness of time, an eventual headache is as may be.

Precision comes mainly with the measuring of quantities, as the two foregoing examples illustrate. A notable boon of injecting quantity into hypotheses is *concomitant variation,* or *functional dependence.* Change the pressure from 760 millimeters to a lower or higher figure, and you change the boiling point of water from 100°C. to a correspondingly lower or higher figure. Once such a hypothesis is devised, describing the fluctuation of one quantity explicitly as some function of the fluctuation of another quantity, the confirmatory power of a few successful predictions is overwhelming.

Precision sometimes obstructs generality and sometimes not. The hypothesis about the boiling point of water can be generalized to pressures other than 760 millimeters without loss of precision by expressing the boiling point of pure water as an arithmetical function of the pressure. On the other hand if we want to generalize to impure water we must drop some precision, because the effect of impurities upon the boiling point varies not only with their amount but with their nature.

Measure is not the sole source of precision. Another way of increasing precision is redefinition of terms. We take a term that is fuzzy and imprecise and try to sharpen its sense without impairing its usefulness. In so sharpening we may effect changes in the term's application; a new definition may let the term apply to some things that it did not formerly apply to, and it may keep the term from applying to some of the things to which it had applied. The idea is to have any changes come in harmless cases, so that precision is gained without loss. It is to be noted that hypotheses briefly expressible in everyday terms and purporting to have broad application rarely turn out to be unexceptionable. This is even to be expected, since everyday terms are mainly suited for everyday affairs, where lax talk is rife.

When philosophers give a precise sense to what was formerly a fuzzy term or concept it is called *explication* of that term or concept. Successful explications have been found for the concepts of deduction, probability, and computability, to name just three. It is no wonder that philosophers seek explications; for explications are steps toward clarity. But philosophers are not alone in this.

Biologists gained precision and something more when they gave the common term "fish" a sharp definition that banned whales; for the new distinction turned on biological characteristics that entered elsewhere into theory. Physicists made similar gains when they redefined such terms as "momentum" and "energy". Looking in another direction, we find judicial decisions contributing to the sharpening of legal concepts even without recourse to explicit definitions. Decisions regarding contracts, fraud, and conspiracy, for example, may give new guidelines for determining the range of those concepts. In English law the practice is to use old decisions as criteria as long as possible, and then, when old lines fail, to draw finer lines through fresh decisions.

Let us turn back now for a further look at confirmation. Virtues I through VI, though they give reasons to believe a hypothesis, are not called confirmation; this term is used more narrowly, for confirmation in experience. What confirms a hypothesis, insofar as it gets confirmed, is the verification of its predictions. When, more particularly, the hypothesis is a generalization arrived at by induction, those predictions are simply instances of the generalization. Thus what confirm an induction are its instances.

Each green emerald confirms, in its small way, the induction that all emeralds are green.

But not every generalization is confirmed by its instances. This was the lesson of Goodman's contrived example of the grue emeralds. One or a thousand grue emeralds, inspected before the pivotal midnight, count none toward confirming the generalization that all emeralds are grue. Grue is not projectible. "All emeralds are grue" is not fair game for induction. In a word, "All emeralds are grue" is not *lawlike*. A lawlike general sentence is one whose instances count toward its confirmation; hence one couched in projectible predicates. Such sentences are called lawlike, rather than laws, in order not to demand that they be true. "All emeralds are green" and "All emeralds are blue" are equally lawlike, but only the former is true.

At this point a technical refinement is needed. Note that all emeralds are green if and only if all ungreen things are nonemeralds. The two sentences logically imply each other (Chapter IV); they are logically *equivalent.* Surely, then, whatever confirms the one must confirm the other. But "All emeralds are green" is confirmed by its instances, the green emeralds, and these are not instances of "All ungreen things are nonemeralds." The instances of the latter are the ungreen nonemeralds, for instance chickens. Chickens do not confirm "All emeralds are green," nor, therefore, can they be counted as confirming "All ungreen things are nonemeralds." So this sentence fails of lawlikeness, if lawlike sentences are defined simply as general sentences that are confirmed by their instances. Still this conclusion is intolerable, since the sentence is equivalent to the law "All emeralds are green." This quandary was propounded by the contemporary philosopher Carl G. Hempel. A way around it is to widen the definition of lawlikeness by saying that the lawlike sentences comprise not just the general sentences that are confirmed by their instances, but also all logical equivalents of such sentences.

In practice we seem to be able to recognize projectibility to our own satisfaction, and therewith lawlikeness, in most cases. Clear examples of lawlike sentences are "Whenever my toe hurts it rains," "All undergraduate courses have final examinations," "Every hydrogen molecule contains two atoms," and "Intensity of light varies inversely with the square of its source's distance." (Remember that a sentence need not be true to be lawlike.) A pair of sentences closer to borderline might be "All the coins in my pocket on Monday were dimes" and "Every coin I will receive in change next year will have been minted after 1929." The first of this pair appears to fall short of the line, since it is doubtful that verification of any one instance makes any other more likely; the second of the pair could pass as lawlike. Our readiness to draw the distinction in practice, in so many cases, is simply a manifestation of our flair for projectible traits; and we surmised in Chapter VII that this flair is in part an inherited result of evolution.

Typically, still, a lawlike generalization is confirmed by each of its instances. The instance does not of course clinch the generalization, but adds to its plausibility. A generalization with even a single false instance, on the other hand, is irremediably false. Any hypothesis, indeed any statement at all, that implies a falsehood is itself false. This asymmetry is pure logic: what implies a truth may be true or false, but what implies a falsehood is false.

It would appear to be easier, therefore, to refute a false hypothesis than to establish a true one. If a hypothesis implies observations at all, we may stand ready to drop the hypothesis as false as soon as an observation that it predicts fails to occur. In fact, however, the refutation of hypotheses is not that simple. We already know this from what was said in Chapter VI regarding Virtue V, refutability; there is the matter of the supporting chorus. It is not the contemplated hypothesis alone that does the implying, but rather that hypothesis and a supporting chorus of background beliefs. Nor is it usually a simple observation that is implied, but rather a conditional prediction that if a certain step is taken the observation will ensue. Discarding any particular hypothesis is just one of many ways of maintaining consistency in the face of a contrary observation; there are in principle many alternative ways of setting our beliefs in order.

Thus, consider again the hypothesis that pure water under 760 millimeters pressure boils at 100°C. Suppose that a quantity of what we take to be very pure water under a pressure of very nearly 760 is found to boil at 92°C. What conflict are not merely (a) the hypothesis and (b) the boiling at 92°C. Two further parties to the conflict immediately stand forth: the belief that (c) the water was pure and (d) the pressure was close enough to 760. Discarding the hypothesis is one way of maintaining consistency, but there are other ways. In the imagined case, of course, no scientist would reject the hypothesis, because it is such a highly accredited part of chemistry. Instead he would challenge (b), (c), or (d), each of which is open to question. In fact (b), (c), and (d) each rest in turn on some physics or chemistry, through the methods we use for determining what the temperature and pressure of a given liquid are, and when a liquid comes to a boil, and whether a liquid is pure water. So more than observation has entered into our acceptance of (b), (c), and (d). And even if we question no general beliefs underlying (b), (c), and (d), there could be some mistaken reading of dials and gauges. What has come to grief in our example is a whole family of beliefs. Sometimes when this happens it is relatively clear which

members of the family are best rejected, and sometimes
not—as witness the case of Abbott, Babbitt, and Cabot in
Chapter II.

We often speak of certain observations as consequences
of a hypothesis. However, on more careful study we invariably find them to be consequences not of that hypothesis alone, but of the hypothesis together with other
assumptions that we make. And the more precise the hypothesis the more likely this is; for the tighter its specifications are, the more techniques and previously accepted
beliefs we need in order to see that the specifications are
met. In the hypothesis just considered we needed techniques for determining, *inter alia,* that the water was pure
and the pressure close enough to 760 millimeters. Our
method for showing a hypothesis false turns out to be a
method only for showing that something we have used is
wrong—maybe the hypothesis under test and maybe
some other belief.

Precise hypotheses, we see, are hard to isolate for testing. They tend to carry other beliefs with them. Imprecise
ones, on the other hand, can be hard to test because of
difficulty in determining exactly what they imply. The
pickles hypothesis may be seen as an example of that.
Again "Water boils at 100°C.," taken without its sharp
conditions, must be seen as too incomplete for appraisal,
if not just false outright.

Hypotheses are supported by other hypotheses, and ultimately by observation, some more firmly than others.
Some philosophers of science have tried to apply numerical probabilities as measures of the firmness of support. In
games of chance the probability of hypotheses makes good
sense; in fact, this is where the calculus of probabilities
began. There is a clear reason to assign a probability of 1
in not quite 505 to the hypothesis that your next poker
hand will be a pat flush. It is clear what information to use

in this computation; for we know what cards are in the deck and that you will receive five, while we do not know the order of the cards nor any other influences. This available information consequently reduces the question to a count of combinations. In the wider world, however, how could we begin to calculate the probability of a hypothesis —say of the hypothesis that the universe began with a bang, or that Babbitt was the murderer? There would be the problem of cataloguing all relevant information. Also there would be the far greater problem, which seems hopeless on the face of it, of compartmenting all alternative possibilities into what could be viewed as equal bits, preparatory to counting combinations. For the foreseeable future we can do no better on the whole, regarding the degree of confirmation of our hypotheses, than regard some as better confirmed than others and some as not comparable in those terms at all. This we must all see as the practical situation; and some philosophers see it also as the necessary situation in principle. C. S. Peirce, writing of induction, expressed the point thus:

> It may be conceived, and often is conceived, that induction lends a probability to its conclusion. Now that is not the way in which induction leads to the truth. It lends no definite probability to its conclusion. It is nonsense to talk of the probability of a law, as if we could pick universes out of a grab-bag and find in what proportion of them the law held good ... What induction does (namely, to commence a proceeding which must in the long run approximate to the truth) ... is infinitely more to the purpose.[1]

Cases do sometimes arise, even outside the gambling hells, where we can make reasonable sense of the probability of a hypothesis. Statistics up to now show, let us

---

[1] *Collected Papers*, vol. 2 (Cambridge, Mass.: Harvard, 1932), pp. 499–500.

suppose, that inoculation against some particular disease has been effective in 93 percent of the cases in which it was used. This makes sense of assigning the probability of 93 percent to the hypothesis that Zee, recently inoculated and subsequently exposed, will escape the disease. It makes sense only relative, of course, to an agreed limitation of information; in this it is like the hypothesis of your getting a pat flush in your next hand.

The paradigm case of a hypothesis to which it makes clear sense to assign a probability is one that says of some fairly well specified and observable event that it will occur at some fairly well specified time. Such is the Zee example; such also is the example of your next receiving a flush. The one would be called a prediction and the other a slim chance, but only because the one probability is high and the other low.

There is always the need to decide what background information is to be taken into consideration. Different ways of setting this limitation can give different probabilities. Given that 60 percent of the registered voters in Wolfwhistle County are registered as Democrats, we might take it as 60 percent likely that Mr. Ledgington, known to be registered there, is a Democrat. Given instead that 80 percent of the membership of the National Tycoon Society is registered Republican, and that Ledgington is a member, we come out rather with a probability of 20 percent at best. Given the two data together, and no others, we come out with neither figure; indeed, we are then hard put to it to estimate the probability.

The question—in the general case a forlorn one—of the probability of a hypothesis is not to be confused with the curious matter of a hypothesis of probability: a *statistical hypothesis.* An example of the latter would be the hypothesis that 51 percent of all children born are male, or that inoculations next year will prove 93 percent successful. These statistical hypotheses are of course just numerical hypotheses. Indeed, the second one is essentially just a prediction, which can be pretty well checked in a few years. Hypotheses of the same sort are commonly expressed more vaguely in ordinary language with help of such words as "usually", "many", and "most". But there are also hypotheses in modern physics that are statistical in a more stubborn and less trivial way. The behavior of elementary particles is in certain respects random in principle, according to quantum mechanics. But this is a realm of theory into which, despite its importance, we shall not presume to try to induct the reader.

Chapter IX

Explanation

The immediate utility of a good hypothesis is as an aid to prediction. For it is by predicting the effect of our actions or of other observed events that we are enabled to turn our environment to best advantage. A good hypothesis can serve also, conversely, to gratify our intellectual curiosity by accounting for events already observed. Such curiosity, idle on the face of it, is still utilitarian at one remove; for the hypotheses that we seek in explanation of past observations serve again in the prediction of future ones. Curiosity thus has survival value, despite having killed a cat. It is an appetite that is not quickly appeased. Explanation nourishes a desire for more of the same. We may respond to an explanatory law with a wish for a wider and deeper law to explain that law, and so on out.

Imagine a tribe, isolated enough to be unaffected by what we think of as the history of science, that migrates from an inland place to a seacoast. We may expect the tribesmen to become aware of the tides in short order, and if they are at all observant they will soon notice that the tides and the moon's position are related. In particular, they may find what is true of many coastal places to be true of theirs: that just after the moon is overhead the tide is high. This much is already a law, though by our standards a meagre one. It would be an easy law for them to come upon, given a little observation, and it could be expected to gain confirmation readily. We are assuming that the tribe has settled by a port whose establishment is small—which is to say a port where high tide comes while the moon is high.

If some of our tribesmen are curious and observant they will improve their little law. They will correlate positions of the moon with low tides, and they will learn when to expect high tide while the moon is out of sight. They will notice that the high tide that comes moonlessly is a higher tide than the one with the moon overhead. In time they should recognize that the tides are maximized, both high and low, when the moon is new or full.

Even if they are too artless at first to formulate their discoveries, it should not take many months (or moons) for some of our tribesmen to learn to infer from the moon's position and phase a reasonable approximation of the water level. Then they can make predictions as of how high the water will be when next the moon is full and high. It may take longer for them to discover that there are deviations from their scheme—deviations that we trace to changes in the moon's distance and declination. But though rough, what they have may surely be seen as a law; and with it they have an explanation for the observed tides.

We may see their explanation as less than the best one that might be found, and not only because, at the outset anyway, it is founded on hypotheses that are inexact. For

the explanation leaves unanswered the question of *why*
the moon relates to the tides as it does; it offers no suggestion as to mechanism. (Neither does it make any mention
of the relationship between the sun's position and the
tides, but much of that is covered by attention to the
moon's phases.) Now to ask why the moon and tides are
related is to ask for a further explanation—an explanation
of the law that the tribesmen have discovered. Such further explanation would enhance the one already gained.
If there happens to be one among the tribesmen with the
genius of a Newton, some version of the law of gravitation
might be thought of. Such a law would then explain the
lesser law, and it would also make for a deeper and more
powerful explanation of the tides themselves. Indeed,
given enough data about the masses of the moon, sun,
earth, and sea and their relative positions at given times,
the tidal phenomena would be deducible. Actually there
are problems involved in thus calculating tides; theoreti-
cally derived values can run afoul of the particular con-
tours of ocean beds and beaches and even the flexibility of
the earth. But if we can imagine there to have been a
Newton among the tribesmen, we can also imagine there
to have been capable geologists and oceanographers with
whose help the needed extra factors can have been allowed for in calculation.

Even this degree of success need not be the last word as
far as explanation is concerned. The tribesmen could, like
physicists now, seek an even more powerful law or set of
laws—say a unified field theory—under which the gravitation law might be subsumed in turn. As every parent
can attest, the question "Why?" can still be asked no matter how much of a story has been told.

The law of gravitation was first heralded as explaining
such things as planetary motions, the moon's effect on the

tides, and the law of falling bodies. Later it turned out to have wider applications. It was a step toward a physical science which gave rise to rocket projection, to cite one offshoot. So a clearer picture of explanation can be expected to deepen our understanding of how our knowledge grows.

The relation between an explanatory hypothesis and what it explains seems somewhat like implication; at any rate it transmits plausibility. That is, if someone believed the hypothesis to begin with, he should thereby be inclined to believe also what it purports to explain. However, the resemblance to implication is tenuous. Hypotheses do not always qualify as explanations even of what they imply outright. We recall the doctor's purported explanation, in Moliere's comedy, of why opium induces sleep: it has a *virtus dormitiva.* We cannot accept as an explanation a mere restatement of what was to be explained. Shall we then require an explanation to imply more? But this requirement is inadequate still. "Opium comes from poppies and induces sleep" is no explanation of why opium induces sleep, though it implies something more, namely that it comes from poppies.

What about a general statement and a singular instance thereof: does the one explain the other? Not always. Where it is some event or system of events that is to be explained, explanation has to do with cause. If someone falls ill and wonders whether the recent banquet was the cause, then the news that all the guests fell ill is indeed explanatory. If on the other hand he already knew from the suddenness of the onset that the banquet was the cause, then the news about the other guests is not explanatory; what would be explanatory would be some special hypothesis about the grouse or the oysters. A hypothesis is explanatory of an event insofar as it advances us in our search for its causes. And as the example just considered emphasizes, how far it advances us will partly depend on how much we knew to begin with.

What might count as explanation that Bullwhip Fudgies went up two points on Monday? Tuesday's newspaper could be cited in evidence but not in explanation. The settlement of a strike or the rumor of a merger could be cited in explanation of the rise, and the newspaper can be cited in explanation of something else: of our knowledge of the rise.

We saw from the two opium examples and again from the banquet example that implication need not make for explanation. For a hypothesis to explain something it is not sufficient that it imply it. Moreover, it is not even necessary; for there are statistical hypotheses, which explain without implying. The hypothesis that a person was exposed on some occasion to a contagious disease is acceptable as an explanation of his having contracted it, but happily no firm implication is involved; some who are exposed are spared the consequences. What qualifies the hypothesis as explanatory is just that it suggests a causal connection. Of course, such suggestion might not satisfy us. We may probe on in hopes of learning why this one person, but not his comrades, suffered the consequences of contagion. To do so would be to seek a fuller explanation.

What can we say of cause? Physicists try to isolate some elementary forces of attraction or repulsion, the fewer the better, whose combinations constitute all that happens. Impact, as of billiard balls, is the classical example; later examples are gravitation and magnetism. Numerous chains of such little events of attraction or repulsion of particles lead from one big event to another: from the kicking over of a lamp by Mrs. O'Leary's cow to the Chicago fire. Such is the relation of cause to effect. The event in Mrs. O'Leary's barn is indeed only a partial cause of the fire; if to it we add other events, such as an atmospheric high in the southwest, from which other causal chains also led into flaming Chicago, we build up toward a total cause of the Chicago fire.

The influence of the labor settlement on the Bullwhip stock quotations can likewise be seen as coming down to chains of elementary physical forces. Impacts on the eardrums of a man at the labor negotiation table activate his nervous system in such a way as to cause him to walk to the telephone. Forces along the wire trigger activities in other persons until, what with one thing and another, a higher quotation for Bullwhip is caused to appear on the boards and the ticker tapes. Much had gone on, of course, to prepare the man at the negotiation table to respond to his auditory stimulus as he did, and to prepare others to respond appropriately along the way; there were many contributory causal strands. Still, if the physicists are right, they all consist finally of the elementary physical forces.

We often explain actions in terms of motive and purpose. Though psychology is far less developed as a science than physics, such explanations serve us very well. There is thus no reason to impugn them. But they need not be seen as conflicting with explanations of the physical kind; in fact they are filled out and enhanced by such explanation somewhat as the simple tidal account was enhanced by the law of gravitation. For there is no motivation, no purposive action, without neural impulses to initiate it. These impulses trigger the muscles, and the person galvanizes into action. Even when we cite his loyalty or resentment or lust or cupidity to explain his violent behavior, we can still be conjecturing causal chains of elementary physical forces, though we be neither inclined nor prepared to trace the tiny links of such chains.

When the physicist says of a few elementary forces that
their combinations comprise all action, he is propounding
a resounding hypothesis. Like other hypotheses, it is fallible; and physicists have more than once revised their
reckoning of the elementary forces. The concept of causa-
tion evolves accordingly, and therewith the concept of
explanation. The physicist Lord Kelvin said a century ago
that he never felt he had fully explained a process until
he had explained it in terms of impacts; and most of us
still feel that this is explanation at its best. But impact
must be eked out with some irreducible pulls, gravita-
tional and magnetic, and with some more obscure forces,
so we warp our standard of causality to suit. So, ideally,
explanation discloses past events that are connected by
causal chains to what is being explained, and it tells us
something of those chains. How far back we will look for
antecedent events will depend on what our interests are
and on how deep our curiosity goes. Explanation comes in
all degrees of fullness of detail, but actual analysis of the
causal chains into their component elementary forces is
ordinarily not in point. That would be explanation at its
ultimate extreme.

Causal chains lead into one and the same event from
various quarters. Our particular interest in seeking an
explanation may favor one or another of these quarters to
the exclusion of the rest. If someone taxies to the library,
an explanation might be sought either for his visiting the
library or for his extravagant choice of transportation. An
explanation in the one case is that he needed to check one
last quotation before mailing his manuscript; an explanation in the other case is that the library was soon to close.
The event in the two cases is identical, the taxi ride to the
library; so by way of distinguishing the two cases we
should perhaps say that what is being explained is not the
actual event. We can take a cue from Chapter II, where,

confronted with the question of objects of belief, we took
to speaking not of things believed but of sentences believed true. A similar shift is available here: we can think
of explanations as explanations rather of the truth of sentences. The explanation of the truth of "He went by taxi"
is that the time was short, and the explanation of the truth
of "He visited the library" is that he needed the quotation.
But what qualifies these as explanations, still, is that they
point to causal chains, however unlike, that lead into the
single event of the taxi ride. And again, the chains may
be seen in physical terms. Light rays have been reflected
from an incomplete page of manuscript to the man's eye
and have set up a disturbance in his nervous system.
Other light rays have been reflected from his watch to his
eye and have aggravated the disturbance. Other, earlier
impacts on his nervous system had already disposed it to
respond in quite special ways to these stimulations. Muscles contract and, in less time than it takes to tell it, the
man is on the sidewalk with his thumb and middle finger
in his mouth. A strident note is produced, the sound
waves induce sympathetic vibrations in a taxi driver's
tympanum, and so the causal chains proceed.

An explanation need not actually mention any event
that is connected by a causal chain to what is explained.
"The time was short" is not thus related to "He went by
taxi." What qualifies it as explanatory is that it helps us to
infer something of the nature of the relevant causal chain.

Causal chains extend back and back, ever branching.
One causal chain to the taxi ride issued from the reflected
light off the unfinished page. Another issued from the
light off the watch. There were earlier branches that had
conditioned the man's nervous system with some complex dispositions recognizable as *purposes:* the man
wanted to include the quotation and he wanted to mail the
manuscript before nightfall. Explanations of behavior

that appeal thus to purposes, or reasons, are called *teleo-logical.*

Purpose and cause seem to stand in striking contrast, for the one looks to the future and the other to the past. In the Aristotelian tradition both were called cause, but the unity was only verbal; cause in the modern sense was *efficient* cause, and purpose was *final* cause. But we can find a more substantial unity: a present purpose, however forward-looking, is a present state of a man's organism. It is caused by his heredity, by his training, and by an untold assortment of things that have happened to him early and late. Like everything that happens, it may be regarded as a history ultimately of combinations of elementary physical forces; and the man's activity in executing his purpose is more of the same. We can hold to this despite all the gaps in the genetic, neurological, and psychological accounts of the pertinent mechanisms; it is a matter simply of accepting the objective of theoretical physics, which is to discover the elementary forces whose combinations constitute *all* that happens. If the physicist finds reason to think that her inventory of such forces is incomplete, she will try to correct it; we need not assume that her job is finished. But if we recognize her endeavor as valid, we must prepare to accommodate teleological explanation under the head of efficient cause. We must subsume reasons under causes, the *para que* under the *por que,* the *wozu* under the *warum,* the *what for* under the *how come.*

It is fairly easy, we see, to give at least a sketch to this effect where human agents are concerned. A person's acquisition of a purpose and his or her exercise of it are neural and muscular events along the causal chain, be the microphysical details as they may. Teleological explanation takes on a different cast, however, when we consider the question "Why do we have eyes?" and the answer "To see with," or the question "Why do the willows lean over the water?" and the answer "So that their seeds will float away." What confronts us here is no mere problem of the microphysiological complexity of human purposiveness. The trouble is that there is nobody whose purpose might have been operating anywhere in the causal chain.

One proposed solution has been to assume Someone whose purpose was at work at the beginning of all causal chains. Here is a grand hypothesis, calculated to personalize the impersonal teleological explanations and so to accommodate them under the head of efficient cause after all. It is one of the classical arguments for the existence of God, and is known as the *argument from design*. But it has been widely regarded as unsatisfactory because of problems it raises and leaves open regarding the mechanism of the creation and its overall purpose. Pleading the inscrutability of the ways of God has not appeased our appetite for explanation.

Charles Darwin, then, to the rescue, with his abundantly documented hypothesis of natural selection. The seeing eye can evolve in the vertebrate, and hydrotropism in the willow, with never the intervention of purpose human or divine. Organisms show chance variations over the generations because of a process of genetic "mutation" (which was for Darwin just an unexplained fact). These new traits then tend to be handed down to further generations if they are conducive to survival; otherwise they tend to disappear because their carriers tend to die before reproducing. Thus species that survive are to be expected to exhibit traits conducive to that survival, as with our tree. Darwin's is an exemplary explanatory hypothesis, which appeals to plausible and independently discoverable processes. It became, of course, the cornerstone of modern biology. And it reduces the teleological explanations of biology sweepingly to explanations in the proper causal sense. Easy answers like "To see with" and "So that their seeds will float away" become, thanks to Darwin, interpretable as shorthand allusions to long causal chains of natural selection. So interpreted, they conform after all to the general causal conception of explanation that we have been promoting in these pages.

The hostility aroused by Darwin's theory was no doubt due only in part to the indignity of representing man as descended from other animals, and in part rather to its circumvention of the argument from design.

Sometimes requests for explanation are demands for justification: "Explain yourself!" Even here, to the extent that what is sought is an account of how some action came to be taken, it fits our scheme. The justificatory aspect is simply something additional. Other requests for explanation are not requests for explanation of events at all, but rather for elucidation: "Explain your theory"; "Explain what you just said"; "Explain who she is"; "Explain how the pulleys and ropes are connected." (Notice the variation in locution following "explain".) Also we speak of explanation in mathematics, as when we explain why the sum of the squares of the sine and the cosine must equal 1. This would not be explanation of any event in the physical sense, though if the explanation succeeds there can be the ensuant event of a student's at last seeing that the theorem is a theorem. In this case what is really being explained is why one should accept a certain belief. It is just the giving of cogent reasons.

Explanations in mathematics consist in tracing deductive connections; what is explained is seen to be implied by truths already acquiesced in. Explanation of Kepler's laws of planetary motion by the gravitation law is similarly implicative, at least granted a little information about the planets. Kepler's laws are not themselves events, but their relationship to events is evident enough. And those events, the planetary motions, receive an improved explanation of just the kind we have been stressing when the broader law is brought to bear. That is how it was with the tides. We contended earlier that explanations need not imply what they explain; if they do, though, so much the better for the coherence of our beliefs.

Some writers have seen fit to analyze explanation in a way that does require implication, whereby what explains an event would invariably have licensed its prediction if known beforehand. The main drawback with this view is that it shuns statistical hypotheses as explanatory; they are not implicative, and they are not normally adequate for prediction. Still, explanations that do imply what they explain are the best ones of all.

Explanation can be an important means of supporting a hypothesis. Confirmation of a hypothesis consists in verifying its consequences, but we do well also to look in the other direction and consider what could imply the hypothesis. For the hypothesis inherits the full support of any belief that implies it. Thus it is wise and customary to seek explanation not only for what we already believe true, but also for unproved hypotheses. We are rightly wary of beliefs for which no explanation could be envisaged. The hypothesis of purposeful creation noted above is a case in point.

In general we tend to believe not only that explanations exist, but that ones that would enlighten us exist. We believe, for instance, that crimes have solutions. Solutions to crimes give explanations for them, explanations that meet special requirements: they identify the implicated persons, the methods used in the crime, and often the motives. Now just as some unsolved crimes have only a small number of reasonable suspects, it often happens that when we look for an explanation we reasonably believe that it will be found within certain narrow limits. We believe that one of some small number of conceivable explanations must be right. In this situation, elimination of some of the possibilities increases the plausibility of those that remain. Sometimes even an explanation that was initially held to be implausible is accepted because it explains something that can be explained in no other conceivable way. People have been hanged for want of plausible alternatives.

We see therefore that there can be mutual reinforcement between an explanation and what it explains. Not only does a supposed truth gain credibility if we can think of something that would explain it, but also conversely: an explanation gains credibility if it accounts for something we suppose to be true. Sometimes an explanation has no evidence at all to support it apart from the fact that it would, if true, explain something we want explained; and it can draw high credibility from this source alone. If we think of an ingenious way of explaining one of Harry Houdini's baffling escapes—some ingenious contrivance of sliding panels or a severed link—we are apt to accept it simply because we doubt that any other reasonable contrivance could have done the trick. Such argument from exclusion, or from want of evident alternatives, often inspires more confidence than it deserves; but still it has its place. It seems fair to say that any statement is entitled to at least some increment of credibility from the mere circumstance that it would, if true, explain something for which we have found no other explanation. This accounts, in particular, for the interest in mechanical simulation of physiological or mental processes. The mere fact that the machine produces similar results gives some presumption that the details of the hidden mechanism in the brain or body are significantly similar to the machine.

Argument from want of evident alternatives is, however, one of the most abused argument forms. Often when we "jump to conclusions" we are abusing it; we leap at the first explanatory hypothesis that comes to mind without duly surveying the field. But sometimes the abuse is deliberate. Indeed arguments of this kind are a favorite device of charlatans, if not absolutely indispensable to them. Some purported event is described to us in a way that makes it seem not to fit comfortably with our other beliefs; for example, a discovery that there were rocketlike devices in medieval China. We are pressed to see the event as defying ordinary explanation (such as that the medieval Chinese engaged in rocketry, which they in fact did). Before we know it some overwhelmingly ad hoc and monstrously immodest hypothesis, like a theory of visits from extraterrestrial beings, is thrust upon us. Just see how this would explain the discovery! The same pattern is followed when the claim that some woman has facility in a foreign language she never studied is advanced as inviting a doctrine of reincarnation. Many people are eager to embrace such fantastic theories if only given the slightest excuse; the wiles of the false prophets are well calculated to ensnare them. And so it is that vast cults spring up around tissues of distorted description, inveigling innuendo, and concocted hypothesis—carefully woven webs, we might say, of misbelief.

Persistent reports perhaps of strange apparitions overhead, perhaps of shoals of periwinkles in London streets, invite spurious explanations for want of reasonable ones. Stubborn diseases or social ills invite rash or superstitious measures for want of sound ones. Responsible scientists may remain properly perplexed, whereupon an eager and impatient public hearkens to the irresponsible hypotheses that are so easily generated by uncritical if not unscrupulous minds. The scientists' tiresome cautions and disappointing demurrals are apt to be dismissed as old-fogyism or even as rearguard action on the part of an establishment with vested interests.

There are two basic safeguards against such delusions. One is a healthy skepticism about reports purporting to establish seemingly unlikely events and discoveries. The other, which reinforces and extends the first, is firm regard for the Virtues that make for plausibility of hypotheses.

We must be wary, as Moliere taught us, of explanations couched in fancy language. It is a basic maxim for serious thought that whatever there is to be said can, through perseverence, be said clearly. Something that persistently resists clear expression, far from meriting reverence for its profundity, merits suspicion. Pressing the question "What does this really say?" can reveal that the fancy language masked a featureless face. We should also be wary of explanations that seem to work too well, explanations that seem always to be available. If we can conceive of no way of testing "Whatever God wills happens," then we give no explanation when we call something God's will. If we can conceive of no way of testing which of a person's acts spring from his unconscious desires, then we give no explanation of a person's act when we lay it to his unconscious desires. If a hypothesis is untestable, it cannot tell us anything.

We should be wary of explanations that appeal to motives and character traits. Witness what might be offered as explanations for a man's electing to dedicate himself to some self-sacrificing career in which he serves the needs of others. It might be that his concern for other persons was so overwhelming that such a career was all he could consider, so we might explain his choice in terms of his love for fellow human beings. But it might also be that he suffered from some neurosis that made him afraid to think of himself in what are for most people ordinary ways; so we might explain his choice as a neurotic one. These would seem as diverse as two explanations could be. Yet it is possible that both are correct, or even that some firmer criteria are needed for these psychological terms before an objective decision between the two explanations can be hoped for. What is clear is that the one explanation is sympathetically motivated and the other not. It is a sad fact about our views of others (and perhaps of ourselves) that we are inclined to adopt in such a case just the explanation that fits our prejudices. This is sad because our prejudice is thereby reinforced and our vision narrowed, yet without our having accepted anything false, and so without our story's being liable to refutation.

Attributing motives and character traits to persons as aids in explaining their behavior is legitimate only when such attributions can be regarded as hypotheses open to question in the light of further information. Talk about motives and character traits being as loose as it often is, we may too easily become intransigent about an attribution once it has been made. The belief that someone is a selfish scoundrel, once adopted, may be defended in the face of almost anything the person is seen to do. This, we recall from Chapter VI, is true to an extent of any hypothesis if we are willing to make enough adjustments in our other beliefs, but beyond a point it is folly to do this. Even Virtue I, conservatism, will be on the side of jettisoning a belief when the alternative is to make whole deckloads of one's other beliefs walk the plank. The particular danger in attributions of motives and character traits is the possibility of defending them in almost any circumstances without doing much violence to our other beliefs. The danger, in short, is lack of Virtue V, refutability. Where this virtue is wanting, it becomes questionable how much content the attributions have. Characterological attributions to groups of persons as well as to individuals can be offered as deep truths and as justifications for attitudes and actions even when they are empty.

The moral to draw from these reflections is not, however, that motives and character traits should never be attributed. The psychology of motives and character traits is in its infancy, but there is no call to conspire in arresting its development. The moral to draw is just that the question "What does this really say?" is a good one to ask, especially when attributing motives and character traits.

Chapter X

Persuasion and Evaluation

We noted two basic purposes of language: getting others to do what we want them to, and learning from others what we want to know. The former of these purposes is often concisely served by a command or request; this commonly suffices if the one party loves or fears the other, or is happy to do small favors simply to ease social tensions or out of kindness. In more awkward cases, the use of language in getting people to do what we want them to is more elaborate. We undertake to persuade them that they will gain by doing the thing. We may persuade them of this by offers or threats. Also we may persuade them of advantages that would redound to them quite apart from any reward or reprisal on our part. Our problem in this case is to implant a belief in them. Here, then, is a purpose neatly converse to what we saw as a second basic purpose of language: that of learning something from others. Here the purpose is to get others to learn something.

Such, perhaps, under

> The jungle law
> Of tooth and claw
> That still held sway
> In man's primeval day,

was the original point of convincing others: to get others
to do what was wanted. Teaching, thus motivated, can
diverge sharply from the effort to inculcate one's beliefs
in others, since we may get others to do things by implant-
ing beliefs which we do not share. This is the utility of
lying.

Happily, these deceitful measures are often inhibited by
another ancient force, the force for truthfulness that we
speculated on in Chapter V. This force has prevailed more
in some circles than in others; and it has prevailed fully,
we are glad to say, in the circle to which this little book
is addressed. For this sincere circle, the business of convincing others reduces neatly to the business of convincing others of one's own beliefs.

The purpose of getting people to do things justifies indeed no general effort to propagate our beliefs, even with
deception set aside; for many of our beliefs simply do not
bear on people's action. Still, many of us are happy to go
on propagating our beliefs even when nothing is to be
gained but the sharing of them. Like Chaucer's clerk, we
gladly teach. To convince others of one's beliefs may simply be faced as a general objective, then, with or without
ulterior motive. Such is the proper business of argument.

To maintain our beliefs properly even for home con-
sumption we must attend closely to how they are supported. A healthy garden of beliefs requires well-
nourished roots and tireless pruning. When we want to
get a belief of ours to flourish in someone else's garden, the

question of support is doubled: we have to consider first what support sufficed for it at home and then how much of the same is ready for it in the new setting.

Beliefs typically rest, to change the figure, on further beliefs. Some of these supporting beliefs may record the reports of observations, but often in making a belief acceptable to someone there is no need to cite observations. The person may already share enough of the other supporting beliefs so that merely calling attention to some of the relevant connections will suffice. For instance W. W. Skeat, dean of English etymologists, wrote in his dictionary that he saw no plausible etymological link between *heaven* and its German translation *Himmel.* Nor did he venture any between *ever* and its German translation *immer.* Yet he surely knew perfectly well, not on the Germanic side but on the Celtic side, that *m* regularly changes to *v* in certain circumstances. One wonders whether a mere simultaneous glimpse of these three separately familiar matters might not have sufficed to make him believe that *heaven* and *Himmel* were etymologically connected after all.[1]

We convince someone of something by appealing to beliefs he already holds and by combining these to induce further beliefs in him, step by step, until the belief we wanted finally to inculcate in him is inculcated. The most striking examples of such arguments, no doubt, are mathematical. The beliefs we invoke at the beginning of such an argument may be self-evident truths: this was Euclid's way. But they need not be, so long as they are beliefs our friend already holds.

It may happen for instance that our friend, like Gilbert and Sullivan's modern major general, knows and admires

---

[1] We are indebted to Conrad M. Arensberg for bringing the three together for us.

the Pythagorean theorem. It says that the area of the square built upon the hypotenuse of a right triangle is equal to the sum of the areas of the squares built on the other two sides of the triangle. Seeing his admiration for this little theorem, we eagerly ply him with further good news in the same vein. We tell him that the theorem holds not just for squares but for all shapes equally. As long as the three sides of a right triangle constitute corresponding parts of three figures that are alike in shape, the area of the one figure will be the sum of the areas of the other two. Our friend, though visibly gladdened by this generalization of the Pythagorean theorem, is mathematician enough to ask to see the proof. Following in ancient footsteps, we cite another theorem, one having to do with the proportions between the areas of similar figures. This theorem says that if you measure the distance between any two points in one figure and then measure the distance between the corresponding points in another figure of like shape, the areas of the two figures will be related as the squares of the two distances. This theorem is perhaps not quite self-evident. Moreover, we ourselves perhaps do not happen to see quite how to prove it from self-evident beginnings; but happily we are not required to, for we find that our friend already believes it. Also, as we know, he believes the original Pythagorean theorem; and happily, having these two theorems now in mind, he sees also—what is perhaps not quite self-evident either— that our generalization of the Pythagorean theorem follows from the two. Our task of convincing our friend is now accomplished, and we are free to change the subject or to go about our business.

We see here a difference between persuading and training. If we were instructing a pupil in the generalization of the Pythagorean theorem, and not merely regaling a friend, we would press the pupil regarding the preliminary theorem about proportions between areas of similar

figures. We would not merely acknowledge her acceptance of it and go on from there. Part of our responsibility
to our pupil is to school her in critical and rigorous thinking. We would ask her to prove that preliminary theorem.
If she failed, we would prove it for her even if it meant
some interim homework on our own part.

In an effort merely to persuade someone of something,
on the other hand, it would be presumptuous to argue for
any preliminaries that he already accepts. We do well in
such a case merely to seek a basis of shared beliefs broad
enough to support the belief that we are trying to put over.
We do well to appeal to a common ground of beliefs which
are no more particular and detailed than necessary for
agreement. Such is the *maxim of shallow analysis.* It is no
guide for teachers, we saw, and it is a poor maxim also
when we are assessing our own beliefs. But it is a good
maxim in argument, for it minimizes effort for ourselves
and boredom for our audience.

In mathematical arguments, and likewise in the Skeat
example, the supporting beliefs directly appealed to do not
include reports of observation. On the other hand some
arguments do drive us back to observational data. Now it
should be noticed that the appeal to our observations in
the argumental situation, where we are out to convince
others, is a weaker instrument than it was when we
merely ministered to our own beliefs. The difference is
that when we report an observation, we have the observation and others have only our testimony. Our observation
reaches the other persons at one remove, and that one
remove rubs out the guarantee that may be seen as
stamped on observation. Thus, even though we have solid
ground for a belief, there is this rub when we try to convince others. The distinctive trait of observation is, as we
noted earlier, that all witnesses agree. One way to make
up the difference in decisiveness between our observation
and our reporting of it, then, is to get the skeptic to repeat

the observation with his or her own eyes. But sometimes this is a nuisance that the skeptic will not take on, and sometimes, as in the case of a murder or collision, the observation just does not bear relevant repetition.

Much hinges, therefore, on the credibility of our testimony. In Chapter V we noted what considerations might reasonably govern our credence of other people's testimony; and these apply now in reverse. For one thing there was the question of possible ulterior motives, or conflict of interest. Our testimony gains in credibility insofar as we appear to have nothing substantial to gain by being believed, and perhaps even something to lose. Our testimony gains in credibility also insofar as we have succeeded on past occasions in showing ourselves coolly judicious and moderately skeptical. And our testimony gains in credibility most of all if our past behavior has made it evident that we never attempt to inculcate any beliefs but our own. Just as each of us forms hypotheses about the reliability and credibility of others, so do others form such hypotheses about us; and the best way to insure favorable ones is to earn them.

We have been reflecting on the credibility of our testimony specifically in the domain of observation reports, where testimony is often essential and irreducible because of unrepeatable observations. But trustworthiness has immense practical value elsewhere too, if only as a labor saver; for it implements the maxim of shallow analysis. The more honest and intelligent we are thought to be, the less supporting argument we are apt to have to produce in order to convince someone of something. In an extreme, indeed, such a reputation can be harmful to oneself and others, lulling both parties into inattentiveness to evidence.

Let us now sum up something of the nature of argument. To convince someone of something we work back to beliefs he already holds and argue from them as premises. Perhaps we also insinuate some supporting beliefs, as needed further premises. We may succeed in insinuating a supporting belief simply by stating it, or we may be called on to offer support for it in turn. We aim, of course, for supporting beliefs that the person is readier to adopt than the thing we are trying finally to convince him of. His readiness to adopt what we put to him will depend partly on its intrinsic plausibility and partly on his confidence in us. If in particular a proffered belief is a mere report of our observation, he may accept it routinely; for in accepting it he has to trust only our memory and our moral character and not our judgment. If on the other hand he balks even at our observation report, we may try to get him to do the observing.

Often there is also a negative element to contend with: actual disbelief of some of the needed premises. For dealing with this kind of resistance there are two strategies, which are the same as the strategies for broaching the walls of a mediaeval city: overwhelming and undermining. To overwhelm, we adduce such abundant considerations in favor of our thesis that we end up convincing the man in spite of his conflicting belief. He simply gives up the conflicting belief, deciding that there must have been something wrong with whatever evidence he once supposed he had for it. To undermine, on the other hand, we directly challenge his conflicting belief. If he meets the challenge by mustering an argument in defense of that belief, then we attack the weakest of the supporting beliefs on which he rests that argument. Commonly, of course, a combined strategy of overwhelming and undermining is best of all.

Thus, suppose we are defending our political candidate against one of his critics. Our case for him is that he will reduce taxes, reduce street crime, and put an end to the bribery that is corrupting the urban renewal program. But the critic questions this third premise, citing the candidate's long association with a real-estate broker who was implicated in the bribery scandals. If we adopt the strategy of overwhelming, we do not deny the alleged association. We perhaps adduce other evidence—from the candidate's activities in the city council—which tends to show that he is nevertheless a force against corruption in urban renewal. Also we apply ourselves more energetically to the other two premises. We cite impressive evidence of the candidate's record of motions and votes on budgetary questions, and also impressive figures of the drop in the crime rate when the candidate was head of the Citizens' Committee. Perhaps for good measure we also throw in and defend a new premise: that he will improve the schools.

If, on the other hand, we adopt the strategy of undermining, we produce reasons for believing that the candidate's association with the corrupt broker had after all been neither friendly nor profitable, and that the rumors to the contrary were traceable to the broker herself. If finally we combine both strategies, and do so with a good show of evidence at each point, our candidate may presently count his former critic among his staunch supporters.

It is agreeable to note that in the use of the strategy of undermining there is occasionally a repercussion. What may occasionally happen is that our challenge to the conflicting belief is met by so able a defense that we find ourselves persuaded. In this event we are led to give up the very belief that we originally sought to propagate. This is the best outcome of all, if we like surprises and are bent on learning things. This is a time when the second of the basic purposes of language noted earlier has unexpectedly been fulfilled: the purpose of learning from others.

The desire to be right and the desire to have been right are two desires, and the sooner we separate them the better off we are. The desire to be right is the thirst for truth. On all counts, both practical and theoretical, there is nothing but good to be said for it. The desire to have been right, on the other hand, is the pride that goeth before a fall. It stands in the way of our seeing we were wrong, and thus blocks the progress of our knowledge. Incidentally it plays hob with our credibility rating.

The desire to be right is the unimpeachable member of the pair, but even here a word of caution is in order: being right is not always a sign of right reason, or of being reasonable. One might succeed in drawing two to a flush, but it is still bad poker. The best strategy does not win every time; what makes it best is just that in the long run it promises most.

We would rather, of course, be right than reasonable. We would like to get the flush. But what course could one hope to find that would guarantee being always right? What makes the best strategy reasonable is that it does cause us to be right—our beliefs to be true—more generally than alternative strategies do. When the evidence available points the wrong way, away from the truth, the reasonable person is wrong along with it.

To learn to distinguish the plausible from the implausible is to develop one part of wisdom; it leads as well as anything can toward true belief. But wisdom's better part bids us to remain aware that we have less than the whole truth about even those matters we understand best. Such awareness can never be misplaced, since "the whole truth" about anything is but a fanciful ideal.

We speculated that a primeval purpose of trying to convince people of things was to get them to do what we want them to. We went on to reflect that this harsh purpose was gratefully softened as the world improved; sincerity flowered, and with it the urge to share beliefs for sharing's

sake. There is a domain, however, where the practical
purpose, the influencing of action, continues to stand forth
in very nearly its primeval starkness. This is the domain
of values.

To commend a past act is to urge the hearer to act likewise if occasion arises. To recommend a future act is to
urge that someone do it. To commend or recommend a
product is to urge, nearly enough, that it be coveted. It is
no surprise that the words "command" and "commend"
are identical in origin. Commendations seem to verge on
commands, in contrast to declarations of fact.

But when we try to support our commendation of some
act or object, we argue still for a belief: perhaps that the
tidbit will titillate our interlocutor's palate, or that the
painting or sonata will gratify the eye or ear, or that the
act will have consequences to his or her liking. The contrast thus dwindles between evaluation and belief.

Evaluation and belief are of a piece, in this way, as long
as the value concerned is the value of something only as
a means to some further end which is valued in turn.
Given a liking for the sweet-sour or spicy, or for Pissarro
or Beethoven or the welfare of orphans, we have then only
to inculcate a belief that the thing in hand or the act in
prospect will promote one of those desired ends; the support of the evaluation of the thing or act is simply the
support of a belief in a causal connection. Similarly for
negative values: as long as we are warning against something only for fear of ill consequences, what is afoot is
simply the inculcation of a belief in a causal connection.

To see an evaluation as concerned with a means to an
end is to have a criterion for it. And the clearer the criterion, the more amenable is the evaluation to modes of
assessment appropriate for beliefs generally. Whether
Lefty ought to be the team's shortstop, lefthandedness
notwithstanding, is likely to be seen as a question of what

alignment makes the team strongest. Whether the melons
in the crate are good ones might be settled by attending
to their firmness, coloring, and size, or by eating them.
Whether there ought to be an airport close to town can be
seen as turning in part upon the facts about sonic booms.
Evaluations of various teaching procedures can hinge
upon current theories in the psychology of learning.

It was obvious that we were evaluating in Chapter VI
when we declared what were to be regarded as Virtues—
and what as vices—in the winning and winnowing of
hypotheses. The criterion there, which made certain traits
of hypotheses count as Virtues, was predictive efficacy.
The Virtues distinguished those hypotheses that prove on
the whole to be richest in their verifiable predictions.

The line between evaluation and belief is not sharp, and
neither is that between means and ends. Yet both distinc-
tions can be worth making. The more an evaluation is
seen as an evaluation of some end, the greater is its contrast with belief. Think of aesthetic matters. There is no
disputing about tastes: no disputing in the sense in which
one can dispute beliefs. There is only a training of tastes.
In part it proceeds by emphasizing skillfully selected ele-
ments of an object: by pointing them out or even by artifi-
cially accentuating them on a photograph of the painting
or in the rendering of the music. It is here that the skill
of the critic lies. The literary critic can bring various cun-
ningly interlocking structures into schematic relief and
call attention to various symbolic associations and im-
agery in ways that afford new insights into what is going
on in a literary piece. The thus increased familiarity with
the structure of the aesthetic object can engender a liking,
granted a suitable choice of object in the first place. Such
training is very unlike the deductions, the marshalling of
observations, the assessing of Virtues of hypotheses, that
figure in arguing for a belief.

The rather extravagant sort of aesthetic training that we have just now been picturing is by no means the only avenue to the development of discriminating tastes. Frequent exposure to a potentially rewarding aesthetic object can suffice of itself; the significant internal structures and connections can gradually come to the fore, to an appreciable degree, even without the critic's external aid. Emulation is a factor here: the beginner sees that it is stylish to admire certain paintings or music or literature, so she attends to them and pretends or fancies that she is enjoying them too, and at length the exposure serves to make her enjoyment real.

What, finally, of moral ends? What of the welfare of orphans as something to be desired for itself? Here again there is scope for training, but in this case the sort of training that we first think of is different in principle from training in aesthetic appreciation; it is reward and punishment, like the training of dogs. This is a familiar approach in inculcating not only altruistic traits, such as honesty and kindness, but also conventional behavior: proper manners. Where the training is successful, a transfer takes place: good behavior comes to be gratifying in itself, independently of the reward that had been used to reinforce it, and bad behavior comes to be distasteful independently of the penalty that had been used to discourage it. When the training is not thus successful, penalties are kept in force for the protection of others; and such is the penal code.

There is room also, however, for moral training of a kind similar to training in aesthetic appreciation. The technique there was the selective emphasis of some telling traits of the aesthetic object. Now altruism, similarly, can be encouraged by vividly depicting the suffering that might be relieved by the altruistic act, or the joy that might be conferred. For this kind of training to succeed

there must already be some springs of sympathy to draw
on, but there generally are such; and not just because of
earlier moral training by reward and punishment, but—
as Hume saw—because of sheer inherited instinct.

This brings us back to natural selection. In Chapters VI
and VII we speculated on the role of natural selection in
contributing to the success of our hypotheses. Our standards of simplicity and projectibility have evolved along
lines congenial to prediction, this being favorable to survival: to continuation of the genetic pool. Now the same
is true of fellow feeling and altruistic inclinations: such
traits have surely been favored by natural selection, being
favorable to survival of society. People are thus born with
a moral head start. This, and not training, is probably the
main reason for there being widespread agreement on
basic moral issues, even among very dissimilar peoples.

Selfish interests can sometimes sway moral judgments,
as in the case of the huntsman who values animal life less
highly than human amusement, or the despoiler who values the welfare of the present generation disproportion-
ately more than that of future generations. But there can
be disinterested moral disagreements over abortion, euthanasia, compulsory birth control, eugenic sterilization,
capital punishment. There can be disinterested moral disagreement also regarding degrees of altruism: how much
hardship here and now is worth how much welfare for
someone in how remote a society, even in another species,
or in how far future a generation? Such disagreements can
be stubborn, but there are ways of working at them. Sometimes we can demote the issue, in part, to the level where
we are concerned after all with means rather than ends;
thus we might amass evidence for or against the efficacy
of capital punishment as a deterrent. Sometimes, even
where the relevant facts are already known to both parties, one party can still sway the other by the device of

enhancement of vividness; thus a harrowing illustrative account might break down someone's opposition to euthanasia.

Sometimes a deft analysis can weaken a position by dissociating two considerations one of which had been bolstering the other. Thus suppose someone agrees with us about conserving the environment for the sake of unborn generations, but then appeals to the same consideration—namely, the interests of the unborn—to oppose birth control. In response we might say that we recognize interests not in general of future *possible* people, but of people that there will actually be.

There have been many theories that have sought to provide ultimate grounds for what is morally good or right. Some are religious theories, pure and simple; others have taken human desires or interests as their bedrock. Still others are cast in an abstract vein; Immanuel Kant's, for example, turned on what maxims might admit of universal generalization for all people at all times. Some modern decision theorists are now arguing for a foundation that draws on both the interest theories and the abstract ones; they build on a sophisticated mathematical theory of preference. On the whole theories purporting to offer ultimate grounds for moral appraisal have had their troubles; surely none has commanded anything approaching universal assent.

In trying to adjudicate ultimate moral values we are indeed way out on a limb, but we do what we can. There is consolation in our more cheerful previous reflection: that agreement on basic moral issues is widespread, thanks to natural selection. Utter depravity is rather the exception than the rule.

Suggested Readings

Relatively Elementary:

A. J. Ayer, *The Problem of Knowledge.* Baltimore: Penguin, 1956.

P. W. Bridgman, *The Logic of Modern Physics.* New York: Macmillan, 1927.

J. Bronowski, *The Common Sense of Science.* Cambridge: Harvard, 1953.

N. R. Campbell, *What Is Science?* New York: Dover, 1952.

J. B. Conant, *Science and Common Sense.* New Haven: Yale, 1951.

Pierre Duhem, *The Aim and Structure of Physical Theory.* New York: Atheneum, 1962. (French edition 1914.)

Philipp Frank, *Modern Science and Its Philosophy.* Cambridge: Harvard, 1950.

Martin Gardner, *Fads and Fallacies.* New York: Dover, 1957.

P. T. Geach, *Reason and Argument.* Oxford: Basil Blackwell, 1976.

C. C. Gillispie, *The Edge of Objectivity.* Princeton: Princeton University Press, 1960.

C. G. Hempel, *Philosophy of Natural Science.* Englewood Cliffs, N.J.: Prentice-Hall, 1966.

T. S. Kuhn, *The Structure of Scientific Revolutions.* Chicago: University, 1962.

P. B. Medawar, *Induction and Intuition in Scientific Thought.* Philadelphia: American Philosophical Society, 1969.

M. K. Munitz (ed.), *Theories of the Universe.* Glencoe, Ill.: Free Press, 1957.

C. S. Peirce, *Essays in the Philosophy of Science* (V. Thomas, ed.). New York: Liberal Arts, 1957.

W. V. Quine, *Methods of Logic.* New York: Holt, 1972.

W. V. Quine, *The Ways of Paradox and Other Essays.* Cambridge: Harvard, 1976.

Hans Reichenbach, *The Rise of Scientific Philosophy.* Berkeley: University of California Press, 1951.

Bertrand Russell, *Mysticism and Logic.* New York: Doubleday, 1957. (First published 1917.)

Bertrand Russell, *Human Knowledge.* New York: Simon and Schuster, 1948.

Gilbert Ryle, *Dilemmas.* Cambridge: Cambridge University Press, 1954.

Israel Scheffler, *Conditions of Knowledge.* Chicago: Scott-Foresman, 1965.

Israel Scheffler, *Science and Subjectivity.* New York: Bobbs-Merrill, 1967.

J. J. C. Smart, *Philosophy and Scientific Realism.* London: Routledge and Kegan Paul, 1963.

J. J. C. Smart and Bernard Williams, *Utilitarianism.* Cambridge: Cambridge University Press, 1973.

P. P. Wiener and A. Noland (eds.), *Roots of Scientific Thought.* New York: Basic Books, 1957.

Somewhat More Technical:

H. Feigl and M. Brodbeck (eds.), *Readings in the Philosophy of Science.* New York: Appleton-Century-Crofts, 1953.

Nelson Goodman, *Fact, Fiction, and Forecast.* New York: Bobbs-Merrill, 1973.

N. R. Hanson, *Patterns of Discovery.* Cambridge: Cambridge University Press, 1958.

C. G. Hempel, *Aspects of Scientific Explanation.* New York: Free Press, 1965.

David Hume, *Treatise of Human Nature.* Oxford: Clarendon Press, 1896. (First published 1739.)

Leonard Linsky (ed.), *Semantics and the Philosophy of Language.* Urbana: University of Illinois, 1952.

K. R. Popper, *The Logic of Scientific Discovery*. New York: Basic Books, 1959.

W. V. Quine, *Word and Object*. Cambridge: M.I.T., 1960.

Howard Raiffa, *Decision Analysis*. Reading, Mass.: Addison-Wesley, 1968.

Israel Scheffler, *The Anatomy of Inquiry*. New York: Knopf, 1963.

W. Sellars and J. Hospers, *Readings in Ethical Theory*. New York: Appleton-Century-Crofts, 1952.

M. Weitz (ed.), *Twentieth-Century Philosophy: The Analytic Tradition*. New York: Free Press, 1966.

Glossary

Analogy: An inferential leap, by-passing inductive generalization, whereby one concludes that two things similar in some significant respects are similar in further respects as well. The word also has other uses; it is applied to a common way of learning new terms.

Conditional: A conditional sentence is one of form "if p then q." Logical truth of a conditional sentence attests to a case of logical implication.

Conditioned reflex: A specific response that one has learned to make automatically to a specific stimulus.

Deduction: Reasoning in which a sentence is proved from others by a series of self-evident steps. A deduction is an instance of such reasoning.

Demonstrability: A sentence is demonstrable if it can be deduced from accepted beliefs or stated hypotheses. It is absolutely demonstrable if it can be deduced from self-evident truths alone.

Explication: A precise definition, intended to be philosophically fruitful, for what was formerly a fuzzy term or concept.

Final cause: The purpose of an action, event, or object has been called its final cause. This notion of cause stems from Aristotle.

Hypothesis: A conjecture that is entertained or accepted because it would explain, if it were true, some things already believed. The evidence for a hypothesis is seen in its consequences. The word is also used to mean "premise".

Implication: The well-defined core of implication is logical implication. One sentence logically implies another when the conditional sentence which we get by combining the two in the fashion "if p then q" is logically true. More broadly and vaguely, one sentence is said to imply another whenever, starting with the one sentence plus perhaps some self-evident truths, you can get to the other sentence by a series of self-evident steps.

Inconsistency: A set of sentences is inconsistent if the sentences are logically incompatible and so mutually contradictory.

Induction: The method of framing a general hypothesis by generalizing from known cases to all cases of the kind. An induction is an application of this method.

Lawlike sentence: A general sentence whose instances count toward its confirmation, or a logical equivalent of such a sentence. A lawlike sentence that is true is a law.

Limiting principles: Principles, broadly philosophical in tone, that sweepingly disallow one or another sort of scientific hypothesis.

Logical equivalence: Two sentences are logically equivalent if they logically imply each other.

Logical form: A schema or form containing just logical particles and blanks which yields sentences—its instances—upon replacement of its blanks by suitable words or phrases.

Logical particle: Words that may appear in logical forms, such as "every," "that," "is," "an," "and," "or," "not," "if," "but" and "some." These are already more than are needed for construction of the logical forms.

Logical truth: A sentence is a logical truth when it is an instance of a valid logical form, that is, of a logical form all of whose instances are true.

Observation sentence: A sentence whose whole occasion of affirmation is the intersubjectively observable present occasion, hence a sentence that can be learned ostensively and one to which all speakers of the language assent under the same stimulations.

Ostension: Learning by ostension is learning to associate heard words with objects or situations simultaneously observed; such learning depends on no prior acquisition of language.

Premises: The premises of a deduction are the assumptions, whether believed or merely entertained, from which the deduction proceeds.

Proof procedure: A formal method for establishing validity. The most common proof procedures involve axioms and rules of inference. The keynote of all proof procedures is susceptibility of purported proofs to routine check by inspection of formulas.

Teleology: The study of purpose or design, or of final causes, especially in regard to natural phenomena. Teleological explanations of behavior are explanations that appeal to purposes or reasons.

Validity: A logical form is valid if all its instances are true.

Index

About the Authors

W. V. Quine was born in Akron, Ohio, in 1908. He was graduated in mathematics at Oberlin and received his Ph.D. in philosophy two years later at Harvard. He holds honorary doctorates from Oxford, Lille, Chicago, Washington University, Ohio State, Temple, Akron, and Oberlin, and the Butler Gold Medal from Columbia. He belongs to the British Academy, the National Academy of Sciences, the American Philosophical Society, and the American Academy of Arts and Sciences. He is Edgar Pierce Professor of Philosophy at Harvard, where he has taught since 1936, with interludes for naval duty and for visiting professorships at Oxford, Tokyo, São Paulo, and the Collège de France. Among his fourteen books are *Word and Object, Set Theory and Its Logic, Mathematical Logic, Methods of Logic,* and *The Roots of Reference.*

J. S. Ullian was born in Ann Arbor in 1930. He was graduated in mathematics and philosophy at Harvard and also received his Ph.D. in philosophy from Harvard. He has held teaching positions at Harvard, Stanford, Johns Hopkins, Pennsylvania, the University of Chicago, and the University of California. At present he is professor of Philosophy at Washington University, where he has taught since 1965. He has written extensively on topics in philosophy, logic, and computer science.